DR RANJ

HOW TO GROW UP

AND FEEL AMAZING

Illustrated by
DAVID O'CONNELL

wren
&rook

First published in Great Britain in 2021 by Wren & Rook

ISBN: 978 1 5263 6295 7
E-book ISBN: 978 1 5263 6294 0

10 9 8 7 6 5 4 3

Wren & Rook
An imprint of
Hachette Children's Group
Part of Hodder & Stoughton
Carmelite House
50 Victoria Embankment
London EC4Y 0DZ

An Hachette UK Company
www.hachette.co.uk
www.hachettechildrens.co.uk

Publishing Director: Debbie Foy
Managing Editor: Liza Miller
Senior Editor: Sadie Smith
Art Director: Laura Hambleton
Designed by Sarah Finan

Printed in Italy

CONTENTS

HEY, YOU! YES, YOU!

Thanks so much for picking up this book. I don't know what's led you to cracking open the spine. Maybe you've started to notice some changes in how you feel and what you look like. ('Crikey, what's hair doing there?!') Or perhaps you've heard people using words such as 'hormones' or 'puberty'. Your mum or dad may even have 'accidentally' left this book lying around and – whoops! – left you to discover it.

Regardless of how you got here, **WELCOME!**

This book is about growing up. More specifically, it's about growing up from a boy into a man. It's a confusing time, right? I know there are probably loads of questions whizzing around in your head at the moment. Don't worry, I've got your back. Just keep reading and hopefully I'll answer a lot of them for you.

Before we go any further, let me introduce myself. My name's Ranj and I'm a doctor who specialises in looking after young people (a.k.a. a paediatrician). You might also know me off the TV, but my main job is to care for children and young people in hospital. It took six years of medical school followed by eighteen years working in hospitals to finally get to where I am. All that training and experience means that I've learned a lot about what it's like to be a young person, and about the changes people go through as they grow up.

4

However, my learning started even before then. Because, believe it or not, I was young too once. For me, growing up was a tricky time full of highs and lows. I mean that literally – I was the shortest kid in my class for years and developed much later than everyone else. For a while, I was left wondering if I was ever going to 'become a man'! It was embarrassing at times, but I learned how to live with it until I caught up.

Then there have been times where my mental health wasn't great, and moments when I had big decisions to make about how I wanted to live. More on those later. But the important thing is that I got through them all, and here I am: they've made me the man I am today. All of those experiences have taught me a great deal about growing up. Between that and my medical work, I've seen and experienced most of the things that boys go through. And thankfully, I've even managed to work out how to deal with the challenges we all face. So I've written this book to share some of the lessons I've learned. Dive in and enjoy!

When I first sat down to write this book, I asked myself: What does it actually mean to be a boy? Let alone 'BECOME A MAN'. Some people want boys to speak a certain way, like certain things and wear certain clothes. Men are supposed to be strong, tough, handsome, macho leaders, right?

But that didn't feel like it described me, nor a lot of my male friends. So I went back to square one. Whenever you ask people what a boy is, they start by talking about the physical stuff. Naturally, being a doctor, I began by thinking about biology — the 'BITS AND BOBS' of the human body.

In chapter one, you'll read about your body parts and stuff such as

PUBERTY **HORMONES** AND **FACIAL HAIR.**

However, growing up into a man is about way more than that. As the chapters go on, you'll learn about all the other important things too, such as how to understand our feelings, how to have good relationships with our friends and families, and how to look after our minds and bodies.

Are all boys the same?

Some people think that
every boy should love cars
and wear the colour blue
(pink is for girls, right?).
Well, **NEWSFLASH**: that's
just not true. Boys don't just
look different — we're all into
different things too. Some
boys like building dens and
playing football. Some boys
like art and music.
Some boys like fashion and dance.

In a world where we're often told to feel a
certain way or do certain things, it can be
easy to forget who we actually are. Those
pressures and expectations stop us from
being ourselves. And when we can't be true
to who we are, we become unhappy. I bet
you can think of a time when your mates
made you feel weird for liking something,
so you pretended you were joking — and
I'm sure it didn't feel good. Let's break
this down a bit more ...

You may have heard of a pop star called
JESSIE J. She's incredible. I mean, what

a voice! She's sung loads of famous songs, but one of my all-time favourites is called 'WHO YOU ARE'. There's a particular line at the end of the chorus that says: 'JUST BE TRUE TO WHO YOU ARE'. Jessie, you are so right!

Being a boy isn't defined by how you look, behave or whether you like certain things. It's not about where you come from or what clothes you wear. It's not about what colour you like, what your hobbies are, or what you want to be when you grow up. It's also not about who you fancy or fall in love with. You don't have to be any particular way. EVERYONE IS DIFFERENT, so just be true to who you are.

So what does it mean to 'be a boy'? Well, it means anything you want it to be! At the end of the day, you get to decide. As long as you're happy and a good person, you can be just the way you are!

YOU DO YOU

You're probably thinking:

ERM, RANJ, I HAVE NO IDEA WHO I AM YET.

Don't worry. Figuring that out is what growing up is all about. That's what makes it so exciting – you're discovering who you are. And if you embark on that journey by always trying to be true to yourself, you won't go wrong.

I'm going to be honest with you, though: growing up isn't always easy. There will be good times and bad times. There's another line in that Jessie J song where she says: 'It's OK not to be OK'. She hit the nail on the head again!

You see, you don't have to feel happy all the time. In order to appreciate the good times, sometimes you have to see what the not-so-good times feel like. You're not alone – everyone growing up feels like this. So I've got lots of ideas about how you can find your way back to your happy place, whether you figure it out on your own or if you reach out to someone else to cheer you up.

Right. Enough of the serious stuff for now. It's time to get going!

LET'S GET STARTED!

This book is going to help you become **THE BOY**, and **THE MAN**, that you want to be. We're going to explore all the different parts of growing up and explain the things that you're going to go through.

We'll talk about how your body and mind are going to change and how to look after them. We'll chat about your feelings and emotions and how to deal with them. We'll also learn about relationships. By that I mean how you relate to other people: friends, family and those you might fancy (when you feel ready). We'll even cover things such as social media and the Internet because, let's face it, it's going to be a big part of your life even if it isn't already.

My hope is that this book will give you lots of information and ideas on how to be the best you – **HOW TO GROW UP HAPPY!**

As we go on, you'll also notice that every chapter starts with a song. I'm really into my music – in fact, nothing makes me happier than belting out a tune in the shower every morning. So I decided to pick out some awesome songs for you to listen to that go with the theme of each chapter. It wasn't easy though ... there are so many good songs to choose from!

READY?
LETS GO!

Ranj

1

Let's start with a song from one of my favourite
films of all time: *THE GREATEST SHOWMAN*.
Hugh Jackman plays a man who sets up a circus
filled with performers of all shapes and sizes,
each with their own unique talents. The moral
of the story is that no matter who you are, or
what you look like, there's a place for you
in the world.

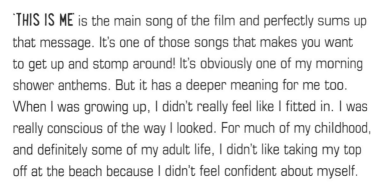

'THIS IS ME' is the main song of the film and perfectly sums up
that message. It's one of those songs that makes you want
to get up and stomp around! It's obviously one of my morning
shower anthems. But it has a deeper meaning for me too.
When I was growing up, I didn't really feel like I fitted in. I was
really conscious of the way I looked. For much of my childhood,
and definitely some of my adult life, I didn't like taking my top
off at the beach because I didn't feel confident about myself.

It's a pretty common feeling. But you know what I finally
figured out? My body is **AMAZING**. You're probably thinking:

BLIMEY, RANJ IS PRETTY FULL OF HIMSELF.
But guess what? **YOUR BODY IS AMAZING TOO.**
If there's one thing I learned when I trained to be
a doctor, it's that all of our bodies are **PHENOMENAL.**

YOUR BRILLIANT BODY

In fact, your body is an **INCREDIBLE** machine. It does so much
– a lot of it without you even knowing. Did you know that
today, your heart will beat around 150,000 times? Or that
you'll take around 30,000 breaths? Or that your eyes will
blink around 25,000 times?!

This **AWESOME** machine means you can do loads of awesome
things – such as backflips in the park, chatting to your mum
at the end of a long day, watching movies, running for the
bus at full pelt when you're about to miss it, and demolishing
a sandwich at lunchtime (which your body converts
into energy so you can learn and do
everything at school). Come on! It's
pretty impressive, isn't it?

But your body is much better than any robot.
Unlike other machines, your body is capable of
changing over time. One of the biggest changes
that happens is called **PUBERTY.**

WHAT IS PUBERTY?

Puberty is what we call the time when your body changes from being a child's into an adult's. Usually, this starts between the ages of ten and twelve, but it can be at different times. It happens to everyone; girls tend to start puberty earlier than boys.

Puberty isn't just about the way your body changes on the outside. It also changes your brain and the way you think. You might find your feelings go a bit haywire. So ...

GET READY FOR AN EMOTIONAL ROLLERCOASTER!

You can feel happy one minute and then really moody the next. Don't worry, this is all **NORMAL**.

Puberty gets under way because your body starts to make chemicals called **HORMONES**. You may have heard of some of them, like **OESTROGEN** and **TESTOSTERONE**. Testosterone is the main hormone that boys make, and oestrogen is the main one that girls make. These hormones cause different parts of your body to change into what they will eventually be when you're an adult. For example, testosterone makes you hairier and stronger.

Here's a picture that shows some of these changes.

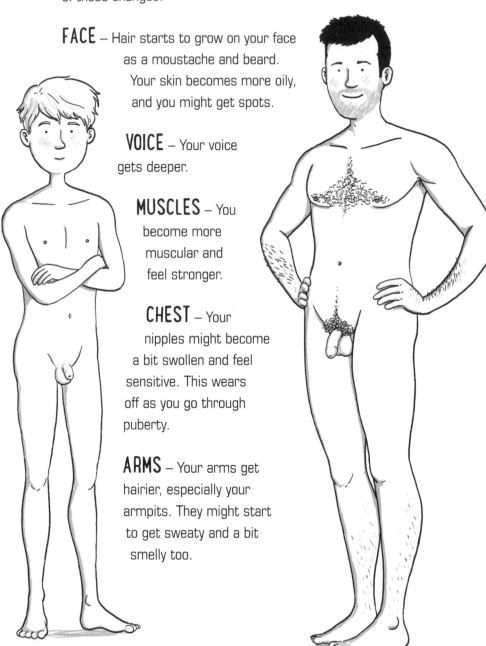

FACE – Hair starts to grow on your face as a moustache and beard. Your skin becomes more oily, and you might get spots.

VOICE – Your voice gets deeper.

MUSCLES – You become more muscular and feel stronger.

CHEST – Your nipples might become a bit swollen and feel sensitive. This wears off as you go through puberty.

ARMS – Your arms get hairier, especially your armpits. They might start to get sweaty and a bit smelly too.

GENITALS – Your penis and testicles will grow bigger and get hairier.

LEGS – Your legs get longer and hairier.

FEET – Your feet will get bigger.

BODY – You will get taller, and your body changes shape. For example, your chest and shoulders get broader.

 ## GROWING PAINS

You might have heard of something called **GROWING PAINS**. These are aches and pains that some people get when they are growing up. We don't really know why they happen. They're not actually anything to do with growing either. They usually happen in the legs and are worse at night-time. However, they're not harmful and will go away by themselves. Taking a warm bath and massaging your legs can help them feel better.

Puberty was stressful for me. My friends all seemed to be developing earlier and more quickly than me and it made me feel like the odd-one-out – I thought I looked so much younger than everyone else. I found it embarrassing to get undressed in a shared changing room for PE, imagining that my friends were all judging me. But it turned out that they really didn't care. And I didn't need to be so worried either – my puberty just happened a bit later. I caught up eventually!

When I was training to be a doctor, I learned that we all grow up at different times and speeds. So if you ever feel like you're lagging behind a bit, try to relax. It'll happen!

ALL ABOUT 'BOY BITS'

WILLIES, DICKS, BALLS, NUTS … yep, they're known by lots of different names, but the proper scientific word for your 'boy bits' is genitals. Your genitals are made up of lots of different parts and each of them has a different job – and some of them are inside your body rather than hanging down on the outside.

Learning about every part of your body is really important if you're going to grow up happy and confident in yourself.

These pictures show what a boy's genitals might look like from the **OUTSIDE**, and also on the **INSIDE**, as well as some of the other organs around.

PENIS
The organ that leads from inside your body to outside.

SCROTUM
A bag that holds your testicles.

FORESKIN
The skin at the end of the penis that is there to protect the glans. Some people have this removed.

GLANS
The sensitive head at the end of the penis (typically covered by the foreskin). You might notice some little spots on your glans. These are called penile papules and are completely normal.

PROSTATE

A gland that sits at the bottom of the bladder and makes fluid for sperm to travel in.

BLADDER

A bag that stores urine until it is ready to come out.

RECTUM

Where faeces (poo) is held until it is ready to come out.

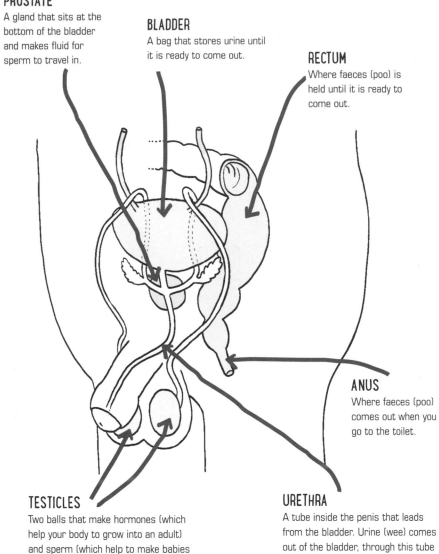

ANUS

Where faeces (poo) comes out when you go to the toilet.

TESTICLES

Two balls that make hormones (which help your body to grow into an adult) and sperm (which help to make babies – more in chapter four).

URETHRA

A tube inside the penis that leads from the bladder. Urine (wee) comes out of the bladder, through this tube and then out of your body.

FORESKINS

Everyone is born with a **FORESKIN**. However, some boys have it removed, usually when they are very young — this is called circumcision. It's sometimes done for a medical reason (e.g. if it's very tight), perhaps because of your religion (e.g. the Jewish or Muslim faiths), or (later in life) simply because you choose to. Not having a foreskin can make the penis a bit less sensitive, but shouldn't affect how it works.

Does size matter?

SOME BOYS ARE OBSESSED WITH HOW BIG THEIR PENIS IS.

They'll be measuring it and bragging about how long it is — even though most of them will probably be making their measurements up. There'll be lots of talk about how big it should be, but in reality there is no point comparing because everyone is different.

I'll let you into a secret: despite what some boys might say, the average penis size is smaller than people think. So pay no attention to the braggers. Besides, your penis will change shape and size as you grow up and depending on lots of things, such as how cold it is and if you're excited.

Everyone's genitals look different, and they come in all sorts of shapes and sizes – most people will be happy with the way they are when they've finished growing. But if this is still something that's worrying you a lot, a chat with your doctor should help.

Embarrassing erections

A boy's penis is usually soft and floppy, but now and again it becomes hard and sticks out. You might have noticed it forcing your trousers to stick out like a tent! This is called an **ERECTION**, though some people call it a **HARD-ON** or **STIFFY**. It happens because blood flows into the penis and fills it up, making it go stiff.

Erections can occur at any age, but get more common during and after puberty thanks to hormones. They usually happen when you touch your penis. You may have already discovered this because you can't keep your hands off it! They can also happen if you're excited or are thinking about sex, which we'll talk about more in chapter four. You'll also find that erections are more likely first thing in the morning.

Unfortunately, during puberty, erections can also happen at totally random times, like when you're sitting on the bus. This can get a little bit embarrassing, but don't worry: we've all been there! Strategically crossing your legs or subtly covering it with your bag or a cushion can help to hide it. It also helps to try not to think about your erection, but instead focus on something completely different (LIKE YOUR MATHS HOMEWORK). And if all else fails, excuse yourself and go to the bathroom until it settles down.

When you have an **ERECTION**, your urethra gets squashed, which means you can't wee. You can pee normally again once the erection settles down.

FINDING YOUR VOICE

One of the most obvious ways your body changes when you grow up is that your voice deepens.

Your voice is created by something called your **VOICE BOX**. This sits inside your neck at the front – just under your chin. It moves when you speak or sing. (I bet you're feeling it right now to check!)

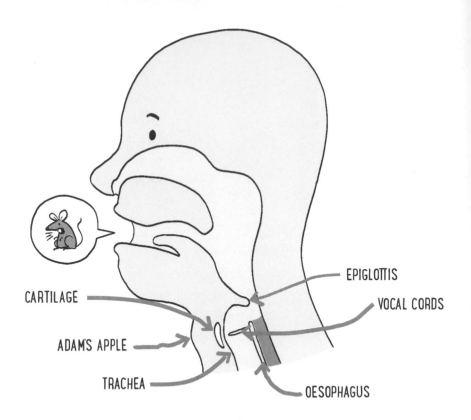

CARTILAGE

EPIGLOTTIS

VOCAL CORDS

ADAM'S APPLE

TRACHEA

OESOPHAGUS

During puberty, testosterone makes your voice box grow. As it gets bigger, your voice will get deeper and will sound more 'manly'. The voice box can start to stick out a bit too – this is what people call your Adam's apple. Not everyone's does, though – mine doesn't!

At first, it can be difficult to control what your voice is doing. You might feel a bit embarrassed about speaking because your pitch can go from **HIGH TO LOW** very quickly (or the other way around, sounding a bit squeaky). Your friends will probably get a kick out of this, but they'll be going through it too. And don't worry, this will soon settle down into a reliably deeper voice.

LOVE THE SKIN YOU'RE IN

Have you noticed that your skin isn't as baby-soft as it used to be? That's because your skin also changes as you grow up, especially on your face.

YOU MIGHT EVEN NOTICE SOME SPOTS

Spots happen because hormones make your skin produce an oily liquid called sebum. This oil comes out of your skin through tiny little holes called pores. If these pores get blocked, boom! You get spots.

Spotlight on spots

Spots can appear anywhere on your body. Usually they happen in areas where you have lots of pores – such as your face, neck, chest and back.

When the pores become blocked, they can look like different colours. If the pore is blocked and closed, it looks white – this is called a **WHITEHEAD**. If it's blocked and open, then it looks dark – this is called a **BLACKHEAD**.

Sometimes the spots can get very red and sore. This is what we call acne and happens because they get infected by germs called bacteria that live naturally on your skin.

I've been really lucky because I've never had acne. But people who do get it can feel really self-conscious because of the way it looks. If this happens to you, try to remember that this isn't your fault – it's just puberty in action. Sometimes people try to make fun of you and say it happens if you don't look after your skin properly, but this isn't true. If you have acne and it's getting you down, it's important to speak to someone (such as a doctor or pharmacist) because they can usually suggest a cream or other treatment that may help. And don't forget: it will get better with time. Brad Pitt, one of the most handsome Hollywood actors, had really bad acne growing up – and look at him now. You might not recognise that name, but I'm sure you all know Zoella (Zoe Sugg) who I know through her brother, Joe. She had really bad acne too, but now she does beauty vlogs!

How to look after your skin

Most spots will get better by themselves, and you'll get fewer of them as your body goes through puberty. But now is a good time to learn how to look after your skin.
1) Wash your face every day. Most people do it twice: when they wake up and just before they go to bed.

TYPES OF PIMPLE

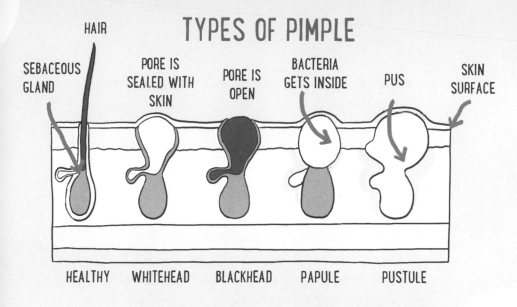

HAIR

SEBACEOUS GLAND

PORE IS SEALED WITH SKIN

PORE IS OPEN

BACTERIA GETS INSIDE

PUS

SKIN SURFACE

HEALTHY WHITEHEAD BLACKHEAD PAPULE PUSTULE

2) You don't have to use anything special. Just warm water and perhaps some face wash is OK. Some people use soap, but this can dry your skin out, so be careful.

3) Dry your face with a towel after washing.

4) If your skin gets too dry, use a simple moisturising cream on it.

5) If you have acne or other skin problems, your doctor may advise you to use special washes or creams. Just follow the instructions.

Even though you might really want to, try not to pick your spots.

OH, I KNOW, ITS SO TEMPTING!

But when you do, they can take longer to heal, and could get infected, leaving you with scars. So even if you're desperate to get the juice out, don't! (OK, if you give in to temptation and do give one a squeeze, make sure to wash your hands before and afterwards.)

SAY HI TO HYGIENE

When boys start puberty, they also get more sweaty, especially in the armpits. Sweat doesn't normally smell, but it can if bacteria on our skin start feeding on it. So it's important to pay a bit more attention to how you clean yourself – this is what we call good hygiene. Sweating also means that you might have to change your clothes more often and can only wear your favourite T-shirts once before needing to wash them. So be ready to do some extra laundry!

It's a good idea to start washing or showering every day – especially after playing games or sports that make you extra sweaty **(AND SMELLY!)**. Important areas to wash are your armpits, genitals and bottom, as these can be the sweatiest and smelliest parts. Just use a bit of mild soap or shower gel and water to wash away any sweat and bacteria.

You might also notice some whitish-yellowy stuff collecting under the foreskin of your penis. This is called **SMEGMA**. Take extra care to clean your penis properly in the bath or shower to help get rid of this: gently pull the foreskin back and wash under it to clean the smegma away. If your foreskin won't pull back easily, don't force it. If it stays tight, speak to a doctor.

IF YOUR PITS ARE SMELLING A BIT STINKY,

using some deodorant after you shower can help deal with any unwanted smells. This could be a spray, roll-on or stick that you rub on the skin. Feel free to try different types – and different scents – to find the one that you like best.

If you sweat a lot and it's making you self-conscious, then you could try something called an antiperspirant. These are like deodorants, but also stop you sweating so much. If it's really bad, have a chat with your doctor or pharmacist, because there is stronger stuff that we can recommend. I sweat loads – especially from my hands, feet and armpits – because I have a condition called hyperhidrosis. I use a special kind of antiperspirant to stop it.

HAIR EVERYWHERE!

Finally, the last big change: hair!

We actually have hair all over our bodies, though some hairs are so tiny you can't see them. During puberty, we get lots more hair because of, yep, you guessed it, hormones.

You'll start to notice more hair on your face as you get the beginnings of a moustache and beard. At first they'll look a bit patchy! But over time, the patches will get bigger and join up. You'll also get more hair on your chest, in your armpits, on your arms and legs, and around your genitals. The hair on your genitals will look thicker and curlier, and is known as pubic hair. It may even be a slightly different colour (usually darker) than everywhere else.

The art of shaving

You don't need to do anything special to look after all this extra hair – how you look is totally up to you. Sometimes people want to shave their faces, while others choose not to because they like the way it looks or because they follow a certain religion. However, some schools do put rules in place about facial hair.

I started shaving when I was fifteen years old and pretty much taught myself. It was about time – when I first started getting a moustache, I had it for ages before I figured out how to shave.

I LOOKED LIKE A LITTLE OLD MAN!

Thankfully, you can all now benefit from my hard-won experience. Here are my top tips for shaving with a wet razor:

1 Get yourself a razor. It should be new and clean and only you should use it. Ideally, get a razor that has safety bars on it so you don't cut yourself too easily.

2 When you're doing this for the first time, it might be better to do it with an adult present so they can check you're doing it right and help out if needed.

3 Wet your face. Cover the skin around your mouth and your beard area with a layer of shaving foam or gel.

4 Wet the razor in some water and then slide it along the skin slowly and carefully in the direction the hair is growing. Going against the hair direction can give you spots.

5 After each stroke, rinse the razor off with some water and then repeat step 4.

6 Take extra care in places where you might accidentally cut yourself (e.g. near the lips or on parts of the face that are spotty). If you do cut yourself, use a bit of tissue to stop the bleeding, or put a plaster on it.

7 After you're done, wash your face with some water and check for any bits you've missed out. Then dry it all off with a towel.

8 Some people find that shaving dries their skin. You can use an aftershave balm or moisturiser to help.

Of course, you could use an electric shaver instead, which doesn't require any water, and there's less risk of cutting yourself, particularly if you have a lot of spots on your face.

Some adults choose to shave or trim hair on other parts of their bodies too, such as their chest or pubic hair, either because they prefer it or for religious reasons (e.g in the Islamic faith). If you do choose to shave or trim these areas, just be extra-careful you don't cut yourself!

Style it out

Looking after the hair on your head is just as important as everywhere else. That means washing it with shampoo to keep it clean, and perhaps following with a conditioner, if you like, to keep it soft. Wash it whenever it feels dirty or greasy, which may not be every day. If you shampoo your hair too often, it can actually dry it out, leaving it damaged. Also, specific types of hair, such as Afro hair, need looking after a certain way, so make sure you know how to do it (your parents or older siblings should be able to show you how).

I've tried lots of different hairstyles as I've grown up – it's part of the fun of figuring out who you are! Short hair, longer at the front, a side-parting, spiked up. Sometimes I style it in different ways on different days, depending on my mood or what I'm going to be doing. So don't be afraid to experiment with different hairstyles – or just grow it long if you like. Using hair gel, mousse or spray can help you style it, but make sure you read the instructions first and only use the right amount. Too much and it might look a bit strange or feel uncomfortable. Oh, and be careful not to get it in your eyes.

A GUIDE TO GIRLS AND PUBERTY

Now we need to talk about girls for a short minute. Girls' bodies change as they grow up too. When girls start puberty, they make more of the hormone oestrogen, and this changes their bodies in different ways to a boy's body, which mostly changes thanks to testosterone. Puberty also starts a little earlier for girls – around the ages of eight to thirteen. This picture gives you a brief idea of those changes.

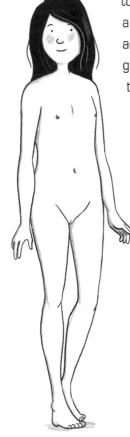

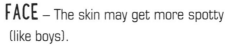

FACE – The skin may get more spotty (like boys).

CHEST – Breasts will develop and grow in size. This can be painful during puberty.

ARMPITS – These get hairier (just like in boys).

HIPS – The hips get wider.

GENITALS – The outside of a girl's genitals (the labia) will get larger, and they get hair around their genitals.

BODY – A girl will generally get bigger and taller (just like boys), and her body might change shape to become more curvy.

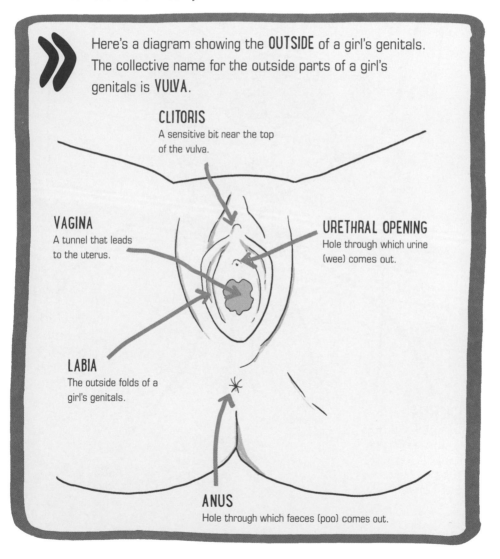

Here's a diagram showing the **OUTSIDE** of a girl's genitals. The collective name for the outside parts of a girl's genitals is **VULVA**.

CLITORIS
A sensitive bit near the top of the vulva.

VAGINA
A tunnel that leads to the uterus.

URETHRAL OPENING
Hole through which urine (wee) comes out.

LABIA
The outside folds of a girl's genitals.

ANUS
Hole through which faeces (poo) comes out.

Here's a diagram showing the **INSIDE** of a girl's body. You'll notice that some parts look similar to those of a boy, and others are very different.

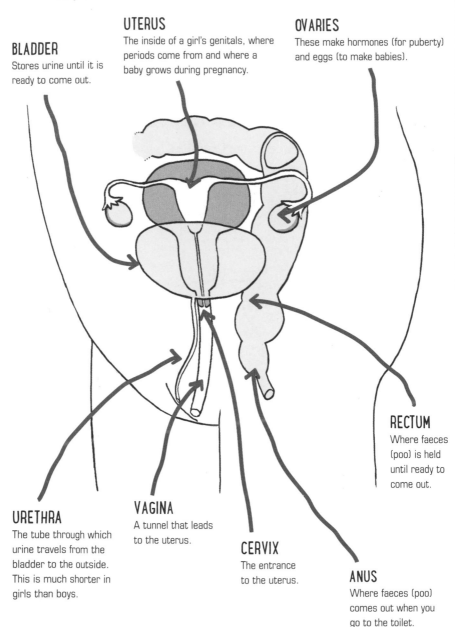

UTERUS
The inside of a girl's genitals, where periods come from and where a baby grows during pregnancy.

OVARIES
These make hormones (for puberty) and eggs (to make babies).

BLADDER
Stores urine until it is ready to come out.

RECTUM
Where faeces (poo) is held until ready to come out.

URETHRA
The tube through which urine travels from the bladder to the outside. This is much shorter in girls than boys.

VAGINA
A tunnel that leads to the uterus.

CERVIX
The entrance to the uterus.

ANUS
Where faeces (poo) comes out when you go to the toilet.

Understanding periods

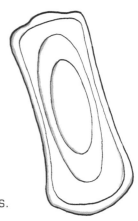

One big difference between puberty in girls and boys is **PERIODS**. You've probably heard the word, and may even think you know a bit about it, but we often hear a lot of myths about periods that aren't necessarily true. So it's important you know the facts.

The hormones that a girl's body produces cause the inside lining of the uterus to get thicker. This is the uterus getting ready for a baby. If the girl doesn't become pregnant, this lining comes away and is released out of the vagina as a period. It contains blood, so looks red/brown. A period happens roughly once every 28 days, then the whole process, called a menstrual cycle, starts all over again.

YES, SOME GIRLS BLEED FROM THEIR VAGINAS EVERY MONTH AND IT'S PERFECTLY NORMAL!

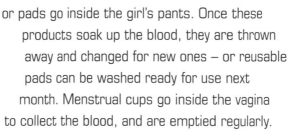

Girls use different products to deal with periods, including tampons, sanitary pads and menstrual cups. Tampons look like little tubes and sit inside the vagina. Sanitary towels or pads go inside the girl's pants. Once these products soak up the blood, they are thrown away and changed for new ones – or reusable pads can be washed ready for use next month. Menstrual cups go inside the vagina to collect the blood, and are emptied regularly.

Even though having periods is completely natural, they aren't always smooth sailing. They can be quite painful, and can also affect a girl's mood because of all the hormones rushing around her body. These symptoms are called premenstrual syndrome, or PMS. Fortunately, it tends to settle down when the period ends, but those symptoms can be horrible for some girls. Being a good friend or sibling during this time can go a long way to making her feel better.

And if you happen to catch sight of a girl's menstrual products in her bag, there's no need to tease her – she's just being organised and prepared for that time of the month.

Girls need understanding too

Going through puberty and all the changes that happen to your body can be embarrassing for both boys and girls. But that doesn't mean you can't talk about it with each other. If you're not sure about how female puberty works, you can always ask a female friend. Just one piece of advice: do it sensitively, and pick the right moment. No one likes to talk about pubic hair in the school-dinner queue!

Even though it happens to everyone, that doesn't stop some boys making fun of girls or making them feel bad for what is happening to them, such as their breasts growing or their periods starting. This isn't right, and it's not fair. How would you like it if someone made fun of what was happening to you? We all need respect and understanding – girls and boys. And if you see someone teasing a girl for it, feel free to step in and stop it. You'll be a hero!

BODY IMAGE AND CONFIDENCE

People think that only girls worry about the way they look. Well, I can tell you that that definitely isn't true. As a doctor, I speak to lots of young people about their feelings and insecurities, and I've noticed that boys have just the same worries.

Growing up, I'd always be looking at other people and asking myself: **AM I NORMAL?** Why am I not as tall as the other boys in my class? How come my body isn't changing like some of my friends' bodies are?

That's when I had to remind myself that we don't have to be like anyone else. If everyone looked the same, the world would be really boring!

When we look in the mirror, our reflection can make us feel a certain way. This is what we mean by body image – it's what you see and how you feel about it, and it can be good (positive) or bad (negative).

Having a healthy, positive body image is really important. It makes us feel good about ourselves. On the other hand, having a negative body image can be really harmful.

It's not easy, though. Every day, we see pictures of people in adverts, TV shows, magazines or online. When we don't look like them, it can make us feel bad, or make us want to try and be more like them. After all, that's the point of adverts! Even now, as a doctor, I still sometimes have those kinds of thoughts: Great hair, great teeth, amazing body … **I WANT TO BE LIKE THAT!**

But each of us is one-of-a-kind. Some of us will grow up to be tall, some of us will be shorter (like me). Some of us will be muscley, and some of us won't. Sure, I'd love to be as tall as **USAIN BOLT** and have a body like his, but I'm not made that way (plus I don't have the time or energy to train like he does)!

It's much more important to look after your body and love it because **ITS ALREADY AMAZING.** So even though you might be different, try to be positive about your body. We are all unique, and we are just as good as each other!

Confidence is key

Your body image can also affect your confidence. If you're worrying about how you look, you may not want to get involved in fun activities or wear certain things.

Trust me, I know exactly how that feels. Do you remember when I said I never used to take my top off at the beach? That was because I didn't feel confident. But then I realised that my worries were coming from my own mind and how I saw myself, not what everyone else thought when they looked at me.

I've slowly learned to accept myself and to not let my feelings stop me from having fun. Now I'm happy to take my top off if it means I get to enjoy myself more. If you learn to love the body you're in, you can be confident too!

If you're struggling with this kind of stuff, talk to an adult, because they may be able to help you feel better. However grown-ups aren't mind-readers, so they'll need you to tell them how you're feeling! Don't feel embarrassed about this – worrying about the way you look is normal, even though you almost certainly don't need to.

And remember: How you look doesn't decide who you are or what you're good at. You get to decide that.

So start deciding how amazing you are right now!

HAKUNA
MATATA!

2

I adore the song 'Hakuna Matata' from the Disney movie *The Lion King*. You know the one, where Timon and Pumbaa tell Simba to stop worrying? It's a phrase from the African language Swahili, and means 'no problems' or 'no troubles'. I've always loved the message – and it was definitely one I needed to hear when I was younger. I even say it to myself now: Stop worrying, Ranj!

Let's talk about feelings ...

There were times growing up when I felt amazing. Like when I played football at lunchtime, or went to science club after school, or had birthday parties at the weekend. But I remember stressing out a lot too. Over school and exams, over homework, over making friends, over how I looked.

Feeling good and feeling low at different times is normal. And you don't just bounce between those two, there's a whole range of emotions that can overwhelm you: happiness,

sadness, anger, frustration, confusion, excitement, worry ...
What's important is learning how to manage those feelings
so they don't get out of control.

So that's what we're going to focus on in this chapter –
starting with where emotions come from.

WHAT ARE THOUGHTS AND FEELINGS?

Scientists have spent years and years trying to understand
how we think and how we feel emotions. In medical school,
I learned that it's all down to some pretty cool stuff that
happens in the brain. **I SPENT THE BEST PART OF A YEAR
EXAMINING RATS' BRAINS!** It was pretty gross, but it taught
me a lot.

Our brains are complicated things made up of lots of
different parts. Each part does a different job. For example,
the back of your brain controls balance, while the front of
your brain is where you do a lot of your important thinking.

There's also a part of your brain where you experience
feelings and emotions. It's called the **AMYGDALA**, and it plays
a really big role when you're growing up. To find out how, we
need to have a little lesson about the brain.

Brainy business

Our brains are like incredible **SUPERCOMPUTERS**, they send and receive information at lightning-fast speeds. And the circuitry of this computer is made up of millions of nerve cells, which carry electrical and chemical signals.

These cells are organised into different parts, which can be divided up into three main sections. It's almost like having three different brains: the hindbrain, midbrain and forebrain. The hindbrain is what we have in common with other animals and controls basic things such as balance, breathing and your heartbeat. The midbrain, as well as doing other things, connects the hindbrain with the forebrain. And the forebrain is where we do all our important thinking, decision-making and memory formation. This is the part that makes humans different from other animals – and what makes you, **YOU!**

I know that sounds a bit complicated. It took me a while to get my head around it too (ha!). Here's a diagram to help explain.

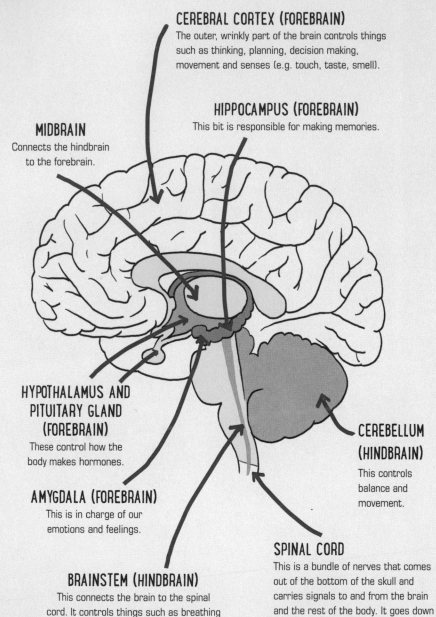

CEREBRAL CORTEX (FOREBRAIN)
The outer, wrinkly part of the brain controls things such as thinking, planning, decision making, movement and senses (e.g. touch, taste, smell).

HIPPOCAMPUS (FOREBRAIN)
This bit is responsible for making memories.

MIDBRAIN
Connects the hindbrain to the forebrain.

HYPOTHALAMUS AND PITUITARY GLAND (FOREBRAIN)
These control how the body makes hormones.

AMYGDALA (FOREBRAIN)
This is in charge of our emotions and feelings.

CEREBELLUM (HINDBRAIN)
This controls balance and movement.

BRAINSTEM (HINDBRAIN)
This connects the brain to the spinal cord. It controls things such as breathing and your heart beating.

SPINAL CORD
This is a bundle of nerves that comes out of the bottom of the skull and carries signals to and from the brain and the rest of the body. It goes down your back inside your spine.

Tidying up ...

As our bodies grow, our brains increase in size too. By the time you turned six, your brain was already about 90 to 95 per cent the size of an adult's brain!

But different parts of the brain develop at different times. So after it has finished growing in size, and putting everything it needs in place, your brain needs to tidy itself up. It's a bit like moving your stuff into a bigger bedroom. After you've got there, you need to sort everything out so it's a bit more organised, don't you? This same process happens in your brain in a very specific order. It starts at the back of the brain first (the hindbrain), and then finishes at the front (the forebrain).

Why is this important? Because it means that the part of your brain that makes logical decisions develops last (and doesn't finish until you're between twenty and thirty years old). In the meantime, you're more likely to rely on other areas such as the amygdala – the bit that deals with all your emotions and feelings. Processing thoughts with the help of your amygdala means you're more likely to use emotions such as love, pain, anger and fear to make choices, rather than thinking them through rationally. And that is what can sometimes make you feel like your emotions are controlling your life – or lead other people to say that you're making rash decisions. But we know your brain is still trying to work itself out.

If you then throw hormones into the mix, which can also affect the way you feel, it's no wonder you go through a whirlwind of emotions during puberty. Don't worry though, you'll quickly learn how to cope with all this and manage your feelings better, which we'll talk more about in the next section.

Things that go
BUMP

Your brain might be awesome, but there are some things it can't do. For example, unlike some other parts of the body, it can't repair itself if it gets damaged.

That's why it's so important to be careful when doing activities that might cause head injuries. So always wear a helmet when you ride your bike! If you do take a hit to the head and feel unwell afterwards, always tell an adult. You might have concussion, which needs to be taken seriously.

MANAGING YOUR EMOTIONS

Have you ever had times when you just feel fed up? Like you
can't be bothered to do anything and just want to be grumpy?
What about days when you wake up, and the sun is shining,
and you're just bursting with joy and excited to start your day?
Or times when something makes you really sad and you just
want to cry?

These feelings are all normal. When you're feeling down,
remember: ITS OK NOT TO BE OK! Whatever you are feeling,
let yourself feel it and don't beat yourself up. Keep reminding
yourself that you can and will feel better — and try to keep
those negative feelings from taking over.

Personally, I find that talking to others really helps me — even
if it's not exactly about what I'm experiencing. Sometimes
a friendly distraction is all it takes to get through it! Others
prefer writing things down, or doing something entirely
different (such as a physical activity). Whatever your
preference, remember that you are not alone.

I've got some more info on how to handle some of the trickier
negative emotions in the next few pages. But as a general
tip, being aware of your emotions can be really helpful. If you
know that you're in a bad mood, or feeling stressed, or feeling
deliriously happy, then you can take that into account when
trying to figure out how to react to challenges and choices that

crop up each day. For example, if your little sister is driving you berserk by following you around constantly, knowing that you're feeling grumpy might help you resist the urge to lash out and say something mean — it might help you be a bit more patient and figure out a different way to handle the situation.

When I'm going through a tough time, one of the things that really helps me keep track of how I'm feeling is my emotions diary. At the end of an eventful day, I write down three different emotions I've felt (such as happy, sad, angry) and why I felt that way. When the emotions are negative, I think about whether there is anything I can do to make it better next time.

HAPPY	My exam results finally came through, and I did better than I thought I would.
EXCITED	I got to order myself some new trainers as a treat for doing well in my exams, and they're going to be delivered in a couple of days.
ANNOYED	I've got more exams in a month, so I have to start revising again soon, but I'm going to make a proper timetable this time to make it easier.

Have a go yourself and see if it helps you feel more in control. There are loads of other ideas throughout this book that can help too. For example, when I'm feeling really upset or stressed, I find something called mindfulness really helpful. Turn to page 135 to find out more.

Seeing RED

Now let's talk about tougher feelings.

ANGER, FRUSTRATION, ANNOYANCE . . . we all know what it's like to feel the rage bubbling up. Well, when you're going through puberty, you may find you experience it a bit more than usual. As a teen, the smallest things would get on my nerves so easily. Usually, that thing was my younger brother. He knew exactly which buttons to press to wind me up.

Whenever I got anything new, such as a video game, he'd kick up a fuss because he didn't get one too. That would drive me up the wall! Why couldn't he just leave me alone and be happy with what he had? Why did he have to spoil it for me? I would get so easily irritated by him, sometimes even angry. I'll bet you've probably felt the same at times.

Why do you feel like this? Because of all the changes that your brain and body are going through right now. Plus there's loads of stuff changing in your life at the moment – new schools, new mates, trying to get your parents to treat you more like a grown-up.

When you think about it, it's not surprising that you get a bit more touchy than usual.

Try not to be too hard on yourself, but see if you can be more in control of your feelings. As difficult as this might be, it's important not to let them get the better of you. Even though you may want to scream at everything, it's never going to help. So if you do find yourself getting angry, try the following:

1) Step away and take yourself out of the situation that's upsetting you.

2) Sit in a calm, quiet place and try to relax. Try closing your eyes and imagining being somewhere where you feel really happy (my happy place is a sunny beach).

3) Focus on your breathing: breathe slowly in through your nose and out through your mouth ten times.

When you've calmed down a bit, remind yourself that anger is probably not the most helpful response. Spend some time organising your thoughts – why has this wound you up so much? What would make it feel better? Is that realistic or fair for everyone else involved? Getting your head straight so you can go back and explain your thoughts calmly will hopefully get the problem sorted out much more quickly and easily.

If you're having a particularly difficult time coping with frustration and anger, find an adult you trust to talk to about it – they can help you figure out other ways to stay calm, or work out what's making everything so challenging at the moment.

BOYS DO CRY

When we talk about controlling emotions, it's important to understand the difference between managing them and ignoring them or bottling them up.

For instance, many boys think that they shouldn't cry or let others know when they're feeling sad. Everyone expects us to be tough and strong. The heroes we see in films are usually macho guys with rippling muscles but no visible emotions. And how many times have you heard the phrase 'man up'? Always needing to seem tough is a pressure that a lot of boys and men feel, and it can lead us to hide how we're really feeling. I wonder if you've ever seen your dad (or uncle) cry? I haven't. In his day, it really wasn't the done thing.

But forcing yourself to suppress your emotions isn't good for you. If you're not showing how you're feeling, you're probably not dealing with it in a way that will help you move forwards either. It can lead to other problems later down the line too. When you're not open with the people close to you, it's hard for those relationships to be as strong as they could be. And if you're trying to pretend that things aren't difficult, then it makes them a lot harder to fix.

The truth is that boys do cry, and there's no reason why they shouldn't if they feel like they need to. Crying can actually help you feel better. After all, if you feel happy, it feels brilliant to laugh. In the same way, if you feel sad, it's perfectly OK to cry. Think of it as an emotional pressure-release button. Once you've let those tears take away some of the super-intense feelings, you'll probably find it easier to think about and deal with whatever is making you so upset.

However, if you find yourself wanting to cry a lot, then speak to someone about it. Maybe what you are feeling is too much for you to handle by yourself. Sharing what you're going through is another brilliant way of helping you process your feelings.

Wrestling with worry

When you've got an exam or a big competition coming up, it's super-normal to feel worried. After all, life is anxiety-inducing sometimes!

Figuring out ways to cope with worry is essential. This is one of my favourite tricks – I call it the **STRESS SAFE**. It's brilliant for helping you get a good night's sleep when you've got something nerve-wracking on your mind.
1) Get yourself a box and some pieces of paper. It could be any box you don't use, such as an old shoe box.
2) Just before going to bed, write down what's worrying you on a piece of paper. Fold the paper up and put it into the box.

3) Use as many pieces of paper as you like for all the worries that are currently getting to you.
4) Put the box away somewhere out of sight. Imagine that this is you putting the worries away so that they can't bother you.

If you like, some time later on, you can take the box out and show the pieces of paper to an adult, and talk through how you're feeling. Usually the issues don't feel so bad then.

One of the things you might be feeling is worry. As we've already seen, it's normal to feel a bit worried sometimes. But if it gets really bad it can turn into something else. When stressful things are going on, your body's natural defence mechanism kicks in because you feel under threat. This mechanism is there to keep you safe and stop you getting hurt, but it can overreact sometimes and get in the way of enjoying your life. This is what people call **ANXIETY**.

Anxiety can feel like intense worry, fear or panic that you can't control. Sometimes it turns up with physical symptoms too, such as a pounding heart, feeling sick or light-headed. When you're feeling overwhelmed with anxiety, try these tips to calm you down:
1) When you feel your anxiety coming on, tell yourself that it will pass and you will feel better.
2) Tell those around you how you're feeling in that moment.
3) Don't get upset with yourself for feeling like you do — it's OK.

4) Try to relax and stay calm as best as you can – perhaps listen to some music or go for a walk.
5) Perhaps try out some mindfulness meditation (see page 135).
6) Don't avoid things that make you anxious, but try to face them as best you can.

I've been there too and these tips have helped me!

I took part in a TV show called **STRICTLY COME DANCING** in 2018. It was a bit of a whirlwind because every week I had to learn a new dance and perform it in front of millions of people watching at home. During rehearsals I found myself getting really anxious, and it affected my ability to perform. But talking about how I was feeling with my awesome dance partner Janette, teaching myself how to relax and calm myself down, and then doing something nice at the end of the day to unwind really helped!

If anxiety starts to feel like it's getting on top of you – like you're worried all of the time, and it's stopping you from getting involved in day-to-day things – then it's really important to speak to someone so they can help you feel less worried. You can feel better!

RISKY BUSINESS

One of the lesser-known effects of hormones and puberty is that, as your brain develops, you'll find yourself wanting to take more **RISKS**. You'll even feel braver about doing certain things. That's great, because it means you'll get to do some really cool stuff such as trying out for a sports team or auditioning for a school play. That's how I ended up working in TV. Being on telly isn't a normal part of a doctor's job, but I came across an advert for a TV channel that was looking for a doctor and I thought: Why not? I'm so glad I took that chance because it's led to loads of amazing things. I now have my own TV show!

So taking risks can be good, but bear in mind that you might also be tempted to do things that you shouldn't. We all feel like being a bit mischievous now and again. Sometimes it feels exciting. Sometimes we're bored. Sometimes we just act on impulse. We've all wanted to push the big red button that says 'DONT PRESS' just to see what happens, haven't we?! (Warning: don't do it!)

Having fun and exploring life is a massive part of growing up, but sometimes the things we do might not be the best idea. In fact, it could land you in trouble if we're talking about breaking the rules or even the law. So when you find yourself tempted to do something that could land you in hot water, take a deep breath and seriously consider the consequences. There's probably a decent reason why there's a rule against you doing it in the first place — and even if not, would the risk be worth it if you got caught?

Sometimes we take risks because we've got other people egging us on. It's another part of that pressure that boys feel to act tough. Some people feel like they have to dress a certain way, hang out with certain people or do things such as drink or smoke, just because their mates are. But don't ever feel like you have to do something just because other people are. Remember, you are your own person.

 ## DO WHAT IS RIGHT FOR YOU

No one says you have to be perfect all the time, but trying not to end up in trouble is going to make your life easier in the long run. So if you're feeling a bit rebellious, try directing that energy into something useful and amazing: dare yourself to try a new hobby or activity that you never thought you'd be capable of. Sport or dance is brilliant for helping you let off steam, while getting into something arty focuses your brain and gives you a creative outlet. And you'll usually meet brilliant mates when you try something new, even if going up to talk to them for the first time feels like the riskiest thing in the world.

YOUR **MIND** MATTERS

You know how everyone bangs on about how important it is to have a healthy body? Well, it's important to have a healthy mind too. This is what we call mental health and it helps keep our minds working properly.

Most of us are able to manage our thoughts and emotions so that they don't stop us doing day-to-day things or cause more serious problems. However, for some people their thoughts can become too much or they might feel things that really aren't helpful.

Some examples of this are:
1) Feeling sad a lot and not being able to enjoy things.
2) Feeling worried a lot or all the time, which stops you from doing things.
3) Feeling bad about food so that you can't eat healthily.
4) Not being able to sleep at night.
5) Feeling like you have to do something over and over again to be safe and calm.
6) Feeling like you might want to hurt yourself or someone else.

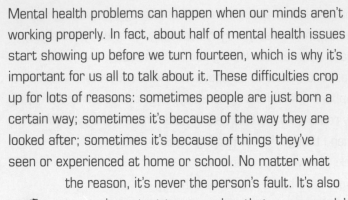

Mental health problems can happen when our minds aren't working properly. In fact, about half of mental health issues start showing up before we turn fourteen, which is why it's important for us all to talk about it. These difficulties crop up for lots of reasons: sometimes people are just born a certain way; sometimes it's because of the way they are looked after; sometimes it's because of things they've seen or experienced at home or school. No matter what the reason, it's never the person's fault. It's also important to remember that some people's brains work in a slightly different way, for example people with ADHD or autism. That doesn't mean they have a mental health problem. Their brain just works differently, which is fine!

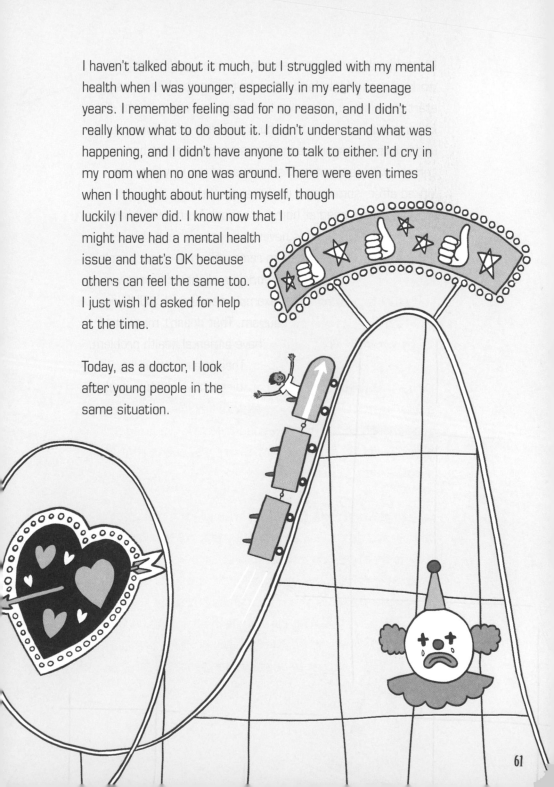

I haven't talked about it much, but I struggled with my mental health when I was younger, especially in my early teenage years. I remember feeling sad for no reason, and I didn't really know what to do about it. I didn't understand what was happening, and I didn't have anyone to talk to either. I'd cry in my room when no one was around. There were even times when I thought about hurting myself, though luckily I never did. I know now that I might have had a mental health issue and that's OK because others can feel the same too. I just wish I'd asked for help at the time.

Today, as a doctor, I look after young people in the same situation.

The key is speaking to someone when you're struggling. It's not always easy to do, but it is the first step to making things better. If any of the thoughts or feeling-patterns in the list earlier feel familiar to you, speak to someone you trust and get help. This person could be a teacher, a member of your family, a counsellor, a doctor or a nurse. There are lots of charities that can help too. There's a list of them on page 154.

Looking after your mental health is really important – just as important as looking after the rest of your body. So there's more information on how to keep your mind in tip-top order in chapter six – along with some exercises to try.

I know that when our feelings and emotions take us on a rollercoaster ride, it can be easy to feel like we aren't good enough and to get down on ourselves. We all do it. I definitely do! Those are the times that we have to remind ourselves how incredible we are.

So, tonight, when you go to bed, have a look out of your window and see if you can see any stars. Try to remember back to that time you zoned out in science class as your teacher droned on about space: stars are huge balls of matter made up of tiny atoms and molecules that are all reacting with each other to produce light. That light travels millions of miles to get to us so we can see them.

Well, the same atoms and molecules that make up stars also make up your body and all the cells inside it. Incredibly, that means you are actually made of the same material as stars. Just remember that whenever you feel like you're not enough …

… YOU ARE STAR STUFF

3

When I was growing up, every Friday evening I would get home from school, grab a big bowl of cereal and watch an episode of *Friends*. It was my end-of-the-school-week tradition. If you don't know what I'm talking about, it's an American TV show about a group of friends who live in New York. Each episode starts with the theme tune by The Rembrandts called 'I'll Be There for You'. It's all about how friends and family are there to support each other – through the good times and the bad.

As human beings, we naturally want to be part of groups. We see it throughout the animal kingdom – just look at a pack of wolves or a school of dolphins! We want to connect with others and feel like we belong, like we are part of something. That's also why friendships are so important to us. However, making and keeping friends isn't always straightforward. So in this chapter, I'm going to explain how to have healthy relationships and when to spot when things might not be going well.

HAVING HEALTHY RELATIONSHIPS

Humans have a natural instinct to form communities because we know they're good for us. And those communities are about so much more than just living together or spending time together. When we have positive relationships with the people around us, we feel safe, secure and good about ourselves. Plus we can help each other out if needed. Those are the bonds that we're talking about when we discuss healthy relationships. Every relationship in your life should be as healthy as possible, from the one you have with your parents to those with your siblings and your mates.

SIGNS OF A HEALTHY RELATIONSHIP INCLUDE:

☺ Feeling happy and safe with that person.
☺ Feeling like you are listened to and can express yourself.
☺ Feeling like they have your best interests at heart, as well as their own.
☺ Feeling like you can trust them, and they can trust you.
☺ Feeling like they would do the same for you as you would for them.

On the flipside, some relationships are **NOT** so good for us. These can be difficult to spot because we don't always realise what's happening when we're in the thick of it. So here are my tips to telling if a relationship or friendship isn't working:

☹ Feeling like you can't be yourself around the other person, or that you have to do things you don't want to do.
☹ Feeling like you're not able to make your own decisions.
☹ Feeling like the other person is making fun of you or putting you down.
☹ Feeling like the other person is using or taking advantage of you for things or money.
☹ Feeling scared or unsafe around them.
☹ If the other person is hurting you in any way.

If you notice any of these, it would be a good idea to talk to that person to see if you can change things. Or, if you feel you can't or it doesn't help, you should talk to someone you can trust about it, such as a teacher or your parents.

WE ARE FAMILY

Our primary relationships are with family, and they are usually the first port of call for most people when they need help or support. They may get on your nerves sometimes, but they mean well ... most of the time!

>> I've got two brothers, and we have a great relationship nowadays, but that hasn't always been the case. My youngest brother would ALWAYS know how to get on my nerves. Sometimes, he'd make the most annoying noises for no reason whatsoever, and it drove me mad! It took a while for us both to grow up and understand each other, but we got there in the end and now things are great. So even if you feel like your family are from another planet right now, it won't always be like that.

No two families are exactly the same. Look around and you'll see so many different kinds. Some of your friends will have one mum and one dad. Some will have just one of either or two mums/dads. Maybe they live with their grandparents or another carer. There will also be kids that have been fostered or adopted and might just be getting to know their families.

FOSTERING is where a young person is being looked after by a different family from their birth family (because theirs can't). It can happen for lots of reasons: their real parent may be unwell, for example. Usually fostering isn't forever – the person might go back to their own family, or to a different one. Meanwhile, **ADOPTION** is where a young person joins another family permanently.

Things can be tough for fostered and adopted kids because of all the changes in their lives. They may not want to move families, but it might be out of their control. Some of them also have to change schools a lot. Some kids have seen and experienced really horrible things. When they move families, it might be a chance for them to start again in a safer place and make new friends. So, if you know someone in that situation show them a bit of kindness – they may not have had many friends along the way.

When parents break up

There will be times when parents have to split up because they can no longer live with each other. It may not be anyone's fault. Sometimes, things just don't work out.

My parents had a really tough time together when I was growing up. They would argue a lot and, even though they didn't in the end, I think they were on the verge of breaking up. Things are better now, but what we all went through was so hard at the time.

Unfortunately, divorce or separation can bring out a side in people that isn't very pleasant. If this happens in your family, you may see or hear things that you don't want to. Neither parent is probably intentionally trying to be mean. It's just that when emotions are high and people are feeling hurt, they can say things that are pretty awful. Try not to let it get to you.

Both **SEPARATION** and **DIVORCE** are difficult for everyone involved. It can be really sad when your parents aren't getting on. You have to try and trust that this is the best decision in the long run. And not everything is going to change – even if they're no longer together, you'll still love your parents and your parents will still love and look after you, no matter what.

Your feelings count too. You might have something to say, but try not to get in between your parents or let their feelings towards each other change how you feel about them.

It's never easy, but here's some advice if your parents are going through this:
1) Try not to get involved in any arguments between your parents. You probably have lots to say, but this can cause more upset to you. Instead, ask them to have their discussions away from you.

2) If it is upsetting you, speak to your parents and explain how you're feeling and what you are going through.

3) Try writing your feelings down. An emotions diary (see page 50) or Stress Safe (see page 54) can be helpful.

4) Remind yourself that this is not your fault. Things not working out between your parents is not because of you, and you can't keep them together. Your parents are not angry with you.

5) Speak to your schoolteacher or counsellor about what is happening at home. They should be able to give you some helpful advice too. If things are really bad, then there are charities that can help (see the resources on page 154).

Blended families

Sometimes when parents break up, they go on to have families with other people. When two parents each with their own families get together to form a new or blended family, their children may find themselves with new siblings they never expected. This can be pretty tough to get your head around. ONE MINUTE YOU'RE THE CENTRE OF ATTENTION AND THE NEXT ALL THESE OTHER PEOPLE HAVE ARRIVED!

If you find yourself in this situation, it's OK to feel a bit upset by it. A part of your world has changed in a major way. It will settle and things will start to feel normal again. If you're really having a tough time, have a chat with your mum or dad about it. There might be things they can do to make the change slightly easier for you. You could also speak to a friend who's been through the same thing. Or maybe your schoolteacher or counsellor?

At the end of the day, it's important that you're happy, but your parent needs to be happy too. That may mean accepting someone else's family into yours. Over time, you'll come to think of your new siblings as new friends (psst! – and new people means new stuff you can borrow ...).

FAMILY FEUDS

Parents just don't understand ...

Do you ever feel like your parents are from a different planet, and they just don't see eye-to-eye with you on anything? I hear you! My parents were a nightmare when I was growing up. They just didn't get what I liked or what mattered to me.

'NO, MUM, I DO NOT WANT TO WEAR THAT HORRIBLE SWEATER OR THOSE TROUSERS THAT LOOK LIKE THEY'RE GRANDAD'S!'

That was usually the point at which I would storm out of the room and sulk.

This is all perfectly normal, and bust-ups with your parents definitely get more common when you're going through puberty. As your brain develops into an adult one, you're getting more of a sense of independence. That means you'll want to make more decisions for yourself – which is an adjustment for everyone to get used to. Although your parents aren't technically from a different planet, they did grow up in a different time. So they may not share the exact same views as you on everything.

Plus, remember how you're more likely to make decisions based on your feelings during puberty, rather than thinking them through fully? Well ... I'm afraid that means that some of your decisions might be a bit **SHONKY**, and that can lead to disagreements too.

However, knowing all that doesn't necessarily help when you're desperate to go out and see your mates, and your parents won't let you. It can be really, really annoying. But I will say this: your parents care for you and have probably got a good reason for what they're doing. Maybe it's getting late, maybe you promised you'd do your homework first, or maybe you've been out a lot this week already? Stepping back and taking some time to understand where your parents are coming from may be helpful. Why not suggest a deal or compromise? You do something for them and you can negotiate something in return for you.

However, that's not to say that your parents are perfect. They're human too, and are dealing with stresses at work and looking after you and everything else. It's not out of the realms of possibility that they might be unfair or unreasonable sometimes, or lose their temper with you when they shouldn't – which SUCKS. Parents get stuff wrong too (even if they don't like to admit it). Use some of the tips we talked about in the last chapter to cope when you're feeling frustrated, and hopefully, when everyone's calmed down, you can sort things out. A nice chat when things have settled is a great way to get your viewpoint across.

No matter how rocky things get, they will get better as you get older – it won't be like this for ever! Your relationship with your parents is one of the most important you'll ever have, so try not to take it for granted. Having said that, I can't tell you how glad I was when I turned 18 and went to university!

>> It doesn't happen very often, but sometimes parents or carers don't have their child's best interests at heart and may even hurt them. If this is happening to you, speak to someone you can trust at school, your doctor or nurse, or a helpline (see page 154). **YOUR HAPPINESS AND SAFETY ARE REALLY PARAMOUNT.**

Sibling rivalry

We all have disagreements with our siblings now and again. It's part of growing up in a family! My brothers and I would end up in fistfights over the silliest things, like who wanted to control what we were watching on TV. It didn't help that we were all similar ages so were all going through the highs and lows of puberty at the same time.

Still, fighting over stuff seldom makes anyone happy. The only way to ensure that no one loses out is to compromise – to come to an agreement where you all get a bit of what you want.

Trying to be mates with your siblings really does help you out in the long run. For example, because we were all boys and of similar age and size, me and my brothers realised that if we got on, we could share things like clothes.

BOOM: JUST LIKE THAT, I TRIPLED MY WARDROBE! (THOUGH TRUST ME, MAKE SURE YOU LOOK AFTER WHAT YOU BORROW — OTHERWISE ALL **HELL** WILL BREAK LOOSE ...)

The kind of relationship you have with your sibling probably depends on whether they're older or younger than you. I may have found my little brother annoying, but he really just wanted a bit of attention because I think he felt left out. On the other hand, you might look at an older sibling and think that they are just so cool that you could never be like them. Take a bit of time to get to know them, and don't bug them if they want a bit of space. They probably haven't got it all figured out even if they seem super-chill.

HERE ARE SOME OF MY TOP TECHNIQUES FOR DEALING
WITH SIBLING SAGAS:

1) Ask them how you can be a better brother, and explain
   how they could be a nicer sibling to you.
2) If your sibling seems really stressed, try not to hassle
   them. Tell them that you are there if they need to talk
   about anything, and let them get on. You can go and do
   something else in the meantime.
3) If you can't work a dispute out between you, suggest that
   you both speak to your parent or carer about it.
4) Always aim to be as fair as possible, and to share as
   much as you can.

The good news is my brothers are like my best friends now.
We can talk about anything because they know everything
about me, and I know everything about them. I'm probably
closer to them than I am to my parents, just because we
get each other so much more! We may have all grown up
and have our own lives now, but we still help each other out
whenever anyone needs it, and I know that I can count on
them to have my back. It's awesome how we have got closer
with time. The moral of the story? Stick with your siblings:
it will be worth it in the end.

Being an only child

Some of my friends were only children. I used to think that they were really lucky, because it meant they didn't have to deal with annoying brothers or sisters, and didn't have to share. But eventually, I realised it can also be quite lonely. At least with my brothers I had someone to chat to or hang out with if I needed.

If you're an only child and sometimes feel a bit isolated, other friends and family can be really great. They can be like the siblings you never had! For instance, I always got on really well with my cousins and they became like extra brothers and sisters to me.

WITH A LITTLE HELP FROM MY FRIENDS

Now, let's talk about friends. Outside of our families, our friends are our lifelines. They're the ones we share day-to-day things with, the people we talk to about school stuff and things we like doing. They're the ones we gossip with. They're also the ones who make us feel like we belong to something.

When things are not going well at home, your friends might be the first people you talk to about it.

This is why it's important to choose the right kind of mates. Having a good circle of friends means things like:

- You have someone to socialise with, speak to and hang out with.
- You can be there for each other if you're going through a tough time.
- You can share games, experiences and birthdays.
- You can look out for each other in case one of you needs help.

You don't just have to be friends with other boys either. Girls aren't an alien species! You're sure to find some that are into the same things that you are. Plus, girls can often be really good to talk to, and they might have a different perspective to the ones you get from your guy friends.

Difference is good!

Accepting differences is an important part of friendship. Not everyone comes from the same type of family, speaks the same language at home or eats the same kind of food.

Some kids at school might wear different clothes to you at home or have a different religion. Some may not look like you because their skin is a different colour or their hair is a different type. Some boys like different things that may not be the same as you. This is what we call diversity.

Having friends from diverse cultures, backgrounds and with different interests is a great thing because you get to learn about life outside of your own and what the real world is like. Some people may have experienced discrimination, or been picked on, because they are different to you. However, **YOU CAN BE THE PERSON WHO CHANGES THAT!** Everyone is equal, everyone matters and we can all get on if we understand that and try to be better.

Remember that everyone deserves to be who they are, be happy and never have to feel bad because of it – that includes you and your friends!

Beware peer pressure

Whilst we all like to feel part of the group, when you're with a bunch of mates, it can sometimes feel like you have to do things just because your friends do or want you to.

EVERYONE WANTS TO FEEL COOL AND 'ONE OF THE BOYS', RIGHT?

You might also be worried that if you don't, you can't be part of the group any more. This is what we call peer pressure and it gets to us all.

It's a bit of a double-whammy, because don't forget that during puberty your brain wants to start taking more risks. This means that you might do something you regret later, and, in the worst cases, this could land you in serious trouble. If this is you, remember that you have your own mind and your own thoughts. You can do what you want to do. Your friends don't always know what is best for you, so trust your instincts if you feel like something isn't right.

Sometimes people use the word 'gang' to describe a group of friends.

GANGS CAN BE GREAT IF THEYRE JUST A BUNCH OF MATES WHO HANG OUT AND LIKE TO HAVE FUN TOGETHER.

But – to get really serious for a minute – some gangs are groups of people who do things that are illegal or that hurt others. This is when gangs are bad news. Members of those gangs might feel like they can't make their own decisions. They might also feel like they have to stay in them otherwise they might be punished. It's important for these people to speak to an adult as soon as possible, or to one of the charities mentioned at the end of the book and get help.

Leave behind loneliness

Everyone feels lonely sometimes, it's not unusual at all. Loneliness is like a warning system built into your brain, telling you that you need to connect to others. The feelings tend to go away when we are around other people that we feel good with. In fact, it's actually a good thing in small doses because it helps you learn how to be comfortable by yourself.

BUT DID YOU KNOW YOU CAN ALSO FEEL LONELY WHEN YOU'RE SURROUNDED BY PEOPLE? If you're part of a group, but you don't feel comfortable or secure in it, that can be lonely too.

Tackling loneliness isn't always easy – it's hard to go out and just make a new friend. I know that first-hand – I often felt quite lonely, and had to make a real effort to find the people who I liked being around and felt at ease with. It doesn't just happen!

There are lots of ways of connecting with other people. So if you are feeling left out, why not try the following:

Being by yourself doesn't have to be a **BAD** thing. Enjoying doing things on your own is a great way to feel more confident in yourself! I always say that good friendships start with being your own best friend! Reading, listening to music, doing crafts or other hobbies are fun and help you relax.

- Connect in person: show an interest in what the people around you are doing. They might then invite you to get involved.
- Connect in clubs: if there's anything you particularly like doing, or are good at, such as a sport or drama, see if there are any clubs outside school you can join where you can share your interests with a bunch of new people. Being part of a team is a great way to feel involved.
- Connect online: if you can't attend clubs in person, check out some groups online (but be careful to only go to official and appropriate sites). Always check the age requirements and if you're not sure, ask your parents if it is OK. And remember that you shouldn't be meeting people in person that you've met online unless an adult knows. There's more information on staying safe online in chapter 5.
- Connect at school: find out if there are any clubs or activities you can join in at school. If there isn't a club for what you're passionate about, why not start one?

Beating bullying

We all know the headlines: bullying is bad. But how do you know when something is bullying rather than just a bit of light-hearted fun? For something that is so often talked about in schools, it can be difficult to spot.

Bullying doesn't just mean physically beating someone up, or making them feel scared or threatened. It involves anything where a person does things to make someone else feel bad. That includes teasing, name-calling and taking someone's things.

Some people get bullied for who they are or the things they like. For others, it might be because they're a little bit different. But bullying is never the fault of the person being bullied. And in truth, bullies often do it because they feel bad about themselves. They may do it because they were bullied, or because they want to feel some sort of power over someone. They might do it because they're actually going through a tough time and it's a cry for help. It's not unusual for both the bullied person and the bully to need help.

No matter what form it takes or why, it is never acceptable to bully someone. So if you're having a bit of an 'uh-oh' moment, thinking you might have done a bit of bullying without realising, you need to stop right now. No one has the right to make somebody else feel bad.

If you've been bullying someone, take a moment to put yourself in their shoes. How would you feel if someone was doing that to you? Is it because there is something bad going on in your life and you're finding it hard to cope? If so, speak to an adult and ask for help. Even if you've behaved badly in the past, that doesn't mean you can't be a better person in the future. We all deserve a second chance.

On the other hand, if you're the one being bullied, your job is not to feel sorry for the bully or to try to change them. But you don't have to put up with it and you should definitely speak to someone about it. All schools have an anti-bullying policy, which is a set of rules designed to put a stop to

bullying. These rules show that the school takes it seriously, but are also written to help the situation without making things worse. There are also charities such as the Anti-Bullying Alliance that can help (see page 154).

OK, so we've talked about the person being bullied and the person doing the bullying. Job done, right? But what about if you see someone being bullied – and you don't do anything about it? I remember someone in my class at school who used to keep to himself a lot. I used to chat with him during lunchtimes just to check he was OK. It turns out he was getting teased a lot by some of the other boys. When I found out, I asked if he wanted me to go with him and speak to a teacher so that we could make it stop. Once the teacher knew what was going on, it soon put an end to the bullying and we became great mates.

When you see something happening, you're what is called a bystander. But if you see bullying going on, you should never just let it happen.

BY SUPPORTING SOMEONE ELSE, YOU'LL HELP THEM HAVE A HAPPIER TIME AT SCHOOL – AND YOU'LL PROBABLY HAVE MADE A BRILLIANT NEW MATE.

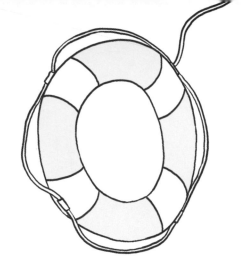

Find your people

Always remember: your friends and your family are there to make you laugh till you cry and give you a hug when the tears are flowing for real. Believe me when I say that the world is FULL of people who can't wait to be mates with you. So, whether it's the sister you can hardly stand at the moment or the quiet guy who lives round the corner, go out and build amazing relationships with the people who are going to be there for you through thick and thin. The people you bond with when you're growing up can be friends for life.

LET'S TALK ABOUT SEX

4

Yup, we're here: the sex chapter. And I've named it after an old song, but bear with me! I think it's time you learned a bit of music history …

Salt-N-Pepa were an American hip-hop girl band from the 1980s, which was when I was growing up. They were loud, in-your-face and all about girl power – and they sold millions of records worldwide. In 1991, they released one of their most famous songs: 'Let's Talk About Sex'!

To this day, it's one of the most iconic songs ever. It's about communication and talking about all the things that no one wants to. It's about being honest and open and, if you don't understand something, being brave enough to ask. That's exactly what I want you to take away from this chapter in our journey. If something is confusing you (especially about sex) and you want to know more, just ask!

What exactly do we mean by sex?

Technically speaking, the word 'sex' can be used in two different ways.

First, it can be used to describe whether someone is male or female (boy or girl). For instance, if you're filling in a form, it might ask what your sex is. Let's talk about that.

When we use the words **SEX** and **GENDER**, we are usually describing whether someone is a boy or girl. In this case, sex is the word which describes which body parts you were born with. Some people call this biological sex. This is something that is decided by your DNA or genes.

Gender is another word you can use to describe whether someone is male or female. However, often people use this to describe what they feel like. So it's more of an identity thing. For the vast majority of people, their sex and gender identity are the same. They feel like the sex they were at birth.

However, for a very small number, their sex and gender identity might be different, and it can take years to be sure. For example, their birth certificate might say they are a boy, but they actually feel like a girl. Or the other way around. This is what we call transgender.

If you are confused about your thoughts and feelings about your identity, your body or your feelings towards others, then it's a good idea to talk to an adult or a doctor.

SEX (THE OTHER MEANING)

The second meaning of the word sex describes taking part in sexual activity or sexual intercourse. This is where two people who care about each other kiss and cuddle and then get their genitals involved. You might think that's a bit gross right now, but we're going to talk about it more over the next few pages.

Why do we need to talk about it?

Sex is a perfectly normal, grown-up, human activity. In fact, are you ready for the most disturbing fact in the whole book?

You are most likely on this planet because your parents had sex! I know, yeeeeesh. I told you, this chapter is all about being honest.

Sex is the reason that the human species exists; it's how we produce more humans. Animals do it too. Some people call sex 'the birds and the bees'. Which is weird, because neither birds nor bees do it like humans, but there you go.

People often get embarrassed or ashamed when they mention sex. Sure, you probably don't need to go around chatting about it willy-nilly, but there's nothing wrong with talking about sex when it matters. It's also nothing to be scared of, though it's absolutely fine if you find it a bit overwhelming to think about right now. Sex might still be a long way off for you.

On the other hand, you might think that you already know loads about it. A lot of people learn about sex from either their friends or from something they see on TV or online. None of these are really reliable, so what you know may not be the whole story.

At some stage you'll be having lessons about relationships and sex at school, which is great. You can use the information in this chapter to fill in any gaps.

I THINK I FANCY YOU!

As you grow up, you'll find yourself developing feelings for others that are about more than friendship. Do you find yourself thinking about them a lot? Do you get a funny feeling in your tummy when you see or think about them? Do you get nervous when you're about to talk to them? Do you want to kiss them? If so, you probably fancy them!

These romantic relationships are part of becoming an adult. Don't panic if you don't feel like starting a relationship any time soon though ... it might just happen later for you or you may not want one at all. I didn't have my first girlfriend until I was nineteen years old. That's probably a bit later than average, but I just didn't feel ready until then, and you might not either.

When someone is attracted to a person of the opposite sex, they are what we call straight or heterosexual. Being gay (or homosexual) means fancying someone of the same sex as you. Two girls that fancy each other are also called lesbians. The collective term LGBT (lesbian, gay, bisexual and transgender) includes those who identify as transgender.

Having strong feelings for people of the same sex as you can just be a normal part of growing up. There may also be times when you have those feelings for people of the opposite sex

too. This doesn't necessarily mean you are either gay or straight. As time goes by, you'll notice a pattern in your feelings and this will give you a better idea of who or what you like. Don't worry about deciding too soon!

There is no rule book about who you should and shouldn't like. You can take your time and see how things go. Some people fancy people of both sexes (that's called bisexual) or don't fancy anyone at all (that's called asexual). All of these are OK! As long as you're trying to be a good person, you're allowed to be whoever you are and love whoever you love. As I like to say: you do you, boo!

Unfortunately, there are some people who are scared of those who aren't straight or of anyone they think is different. They may call them names or even try to hurt them. That's their issue, not yours! Be careful around people who might feel like this, and speak to someone if you ever feel like you're in danger.

Some people use the word 'gay' as an insult. That's never OK. You may have also heard the word 'queer'. Whilst some people see this as a bad word to hurt others, many LGBT+ people now use it to describe themselves in a positive way.

If you've got more questions about this stuff, your school may have a LGBT+ (this stands for lesbian, gay, bisexual, transgender and others) club or society that you could check out. Some schools also celebrate a Diversity Week when they learn about different kinds of people. There are helplines and websites at the end of this book that you can use too.

I realised I was gay when I was around thirty years old – yeah, I know, that's really old! Before that, I fancied and had relationships with girls; I was also married to a girl once. It just took me a while to work out that I probably liked people of the same sex more. When I finally decided to tell others how I was feeling, it wasn't easy. However, my friends and family have been so amazing. Ever since I 'came out' as my true self, my life has got so much better and I have never been happier! I'm so glad I am able to be my complete self now.

Kissing

Kissing is something we do to show our affection. We've all had a kiss on the cheek from a relative or friend. Couples who care deeply for each other, or fancy each other, also kiss on the lips or mouth. Why? Well, there's a few theories about that, but it's most likely because our lips have over a million nerve endings and are one of the most sensitive parts of our bodies. So it feels nice!

If you're going to be someone's boyfriend, then you're probably going to end up kissing them. Kissing for the first time can be a bit awkward, but it's all about trying and seeing what you and your partner like. There is no proper way to kiss and no one nails it perfectly on the first go!

Some people just kiss with their lips. Some people also use their tongues. No matter what your preference, be gentle and take it slowly. It might be a good idea to make sure you have a clean mouth before you do it, though – embrace teeth-brushing!

Want to practise kissing, but not ready to do it with a real person? Why not make a 'mouth' shape using your thumb and forefinger and practise on that?

IF YOU WANT TO BE THE BEST BOYFRIEND IN THE WORLD, THERE ARE SOME SIMPLE RULES TO FOLLOW:

1) Talk to each other and find out what your likes/dislikes are. It's better to get on than argue all the time.
2) Don't forget anniversaries!
3) Listen to each other and respect each other's wishes and boundaries. Knowing what is and isn't OK is a very grown-up way of being in a relationship. Give each other space when you need it, too.
4) Show you care – be romantic, fun and spontaneous!
5) Be willing to come to a compromise when you don't agree on something. You don't have to see eye-to-eye on everything, but thinking of the other person as well as yourself is important.
6) Care for and look out for each other. Keep each other safe.
7) Keep your conversations private. You're likely to tell each other or share very personal things, so respect each other's right to privacy.
8) Be loyal and show the other person that they are important to you. That means not flirting with others!

WILLY TALK

We can't talk about sex without talking about willies – though let's use the proper word, penises. Let's discuss what happens to your penis when you start thinking about sex.

Erections and ejaculation

We talked in chapter one about erections, but here's a quick recap. A boy's penis is usually soft and floppy. But now and again it becomes stiff, especially when they are thinking about sex, feeling excited or aroused (also called 'turned on'), or when they touch their penis.

ERECTIONS happen because the penis fills with blood, making it swell up and get harder. This also makes it look bigger. Blood is flowing around your body and through your penis all the time. During an erection, more blood flows into the penis than flows back out, which is why it gets bigger. Gradually, the blood flows out again and it goes back to being soft.

Erections are designed to get you ready for having sex. If you get an erection and you get more and more excited, it can lead to something called ejaculation. Sperm made in the testicles is mixed with fluid from the prostate gland to make semen – a whitish/yellowy liquid. This then comes through

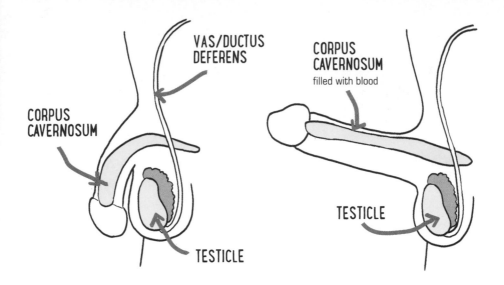

CORPUS
CAVERNOSUM

VAS/DUCTUS
DEFERENS

CORPUS
CAVERNOSUM
filled with blood

TESTICLE

TESTICLE

the urethra and squirts out of the penis during a series of
muscle contractions which you can feel in and around the
bottom of the penis. This release is usually accompanied by
a nice feeling called an orgasm, or 'cumming'.

Girls orgasm or 'cum' during sexual activity too, but don't
ejaculate like this when they do. The muscles around their
genitals will also contract rhythmically. While boys tend to
only orgasm once and then have to have a bit of a break
before they can do it again, girls are sometimes able to have
multiple orgasms.

Masturbation and wet dreams

Some boys like to rub their penis until they ejaculate – this
is called masturbation (or wanking, or jacking/jerking off). It
can feel nice to do this, but don't get too carried away. If you

do it too much, your penis could start feeling pretty sore! Masturbation isn't just for boys – girls make themselves feel good too. However, some people hardly ever masturbate, or don't do it at all, and that's also normal.

There are lots of myths around masturbation, and I've heard them all! For example, one says you'll go blind if you do it. You'll be relieved to hear these are all untrue. Exploring your body is a part of growing up and most adults do it too.

During puberty, boys also often have sexual dreams, causing them to get an erection and even ejaculate in their sleep. We call these wet dreams. They can make a bit of a mess, but aren't anything to be ashamed of. Just wipe up the semen with a tissue and change your pants, pyjamas or bedsheets if you have to.

NOW LET'S ACTUALLY TALK ABOUT SEX

As I said, sex isn't anything to be scared, embarrassed or worried about, though it probably seems like a long way off for you, which is fine. You should only have sex when you are ready and happy to do so. Before you do anything at all, it's important to know what it involves.

When your body goes through puberty, it's preparing you to have sex (and make babies) as an adult. However, sex isn't just for making babies. Many people have sex just because they enjoy it. It's also a way of showing that you really care for your partner.

When a straight couple are about to have sex, they kiss, cuddle and touch each other. The man gets an erection and the woman's vagina releases a slippery fluid. This activity leading up to sexual intercourse is called FOREPLAY and it's important because it gets the partners ready for sex. The man then puts his penis inside the woman's vagina and moves it forwards and backwards. The man may eventually ejaculate (and orgasm), after which the penis becomes soft again and he takes it out. The woman may also orgasm too.

However, it's important to remember that this isn't how everyone has sex. Sex doesn't always involve putting a penis inside a vagina, and it doesn't just happen between a man and a woman. It can also be between two men or two women, albeit slightly differently.

MAKING BABIES

One of the reasons to have sex is when adults want to have a baby. To do this, a sperm (made by the man's testicles) has to come into contact with a woman's egg (made by her ovaries) and fertilise it.

The diagram below shows the stages of development that a fertilised egg goes through in order to develop into a fully formed foetus.

SPERM MEETING EGG
(FERTILISATION)

FERTILISED EGG

2-CELL STAGE

4-CELL STAGE

8-CELL STAGE

16-CELL STAGE

BLASTOCYST

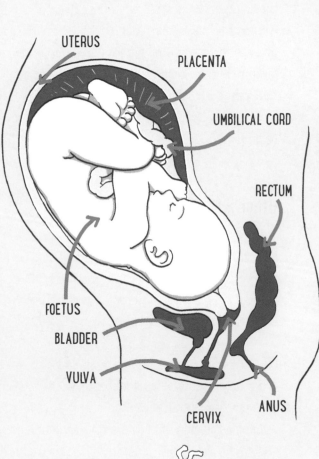

UTERUS

PLACENTA

UMBILICAL CORD

RECTUM

FOETUS

BLADDER

VULVA

CERVIX

ANUS

FOETUS: 4 WEEKS   10 WEEKS   16 WEEKS   20 WEEKS

The egg starts off being released by her ovary and then travels towards the uterus. If the woman has had sex and the man has ejaculated sperm inside her, then the sperm may meet the egg along the way, and one of them will fuse together with it (fertilisation). The egg then buries itself into the lining of the uterus, which has thickened in preparation (remember periods in Chapter 1?). Here it will start to grow to form something called an embryo (one of the names given to a baby inside the womb when it is still in early development). The embryo then develops and grows over a period of about nine months into a baby, and gets ready to be born.

Other ways of having babies

Not all parents make babies by having sex. Sometimes adults may want to have a family but find it difficult or are unable to. For example, a gay couple won't be able to have babies in the usual way. Some other options are:

IVF – When an egg from a woman and a sperm from a man are brought together in a laboratory. The fertilised egg is then put back into the woman's uterus, where hopefully it will implant inside the lining and grow into a baby.

SURROGACY – Where someone volunteers to become pregnant with a baby, but isn't part of the couple who are trying for a family. This person may supply the egg for the pregnancy, or may just carry the fertilised egg provided by the couple. This is all done by IVF.

FOSTERING/ADOPTION – Some people who want to have a baby or start a family will choose to foster or adopt a child (see page 69).

GETTING SEX RIGHT

There are lots of different ways for people who care about each other to feel good and have sex. But there are two really important things that responsible adults should think about when they're getting ready to do it.

Safer sex

If a man and a woman are having sex and he puts his penis inside her vagina, then there is a possibility she could get pregnant – even if he doesn't ejaculate.

However, if they use something called **CONTRACEPTION** then this reduces the chances of the woman getting pregnant. People use contraception if they are having sex for fun and don't want to have a baby.

Some types of contraception can also protect you from unwanted infections called STIs (sexually transmitted infections). STIs, which are passed on through sexual activity, are caused by germs, such as bacteria and viruses, and can give you unpleasant symptoms, or make you really unwell.

When people talk about safe sex or safer sex, they mean using some form of contraception/protection to prevent passing on an STI or avoid pregnancy. LGBT+ people use protection (e.g. condoms) in the same way as heterosexual people, but it's usually to prevent STIs.

THE CONTRACEPTIVE PILL
contains artificial versions of female hormones oestrogen and progesterone, which prevents the ovaries from releasing an egg each month.

IUD a small T-shaped device that's put into your uterus by a doctor or nurse. These release either copper or hormones to prevent pregnancy. Also known as the copper/hormonal coil.

CONTRACEPTIVE IMPLANT
a small flexible plastic rod that's placed under the skin in your upper arm by a doctor or nurse. It releases the hormone progestogen into your bloodstream to prevent pregnancy.

CONDOM thin latex cover that is put over an erect penis and is designed to prevent pregnancy by stopping sperm from meeting an egg. They can also protect against STIs.

DIAPHRAGM a circular dome made of thin, soft silicone that's inserted into the vagina. It covers the cervix so sperm can't get into the uterus to fertilise an egg.

Consent

When two people are kissing, cuddling or having sex, it's really important that they both agree to do it and are happy doing it. This is called consent. Listening to and respecting each other's wishes is part of being a responsible adult.

In the UK, it's technically illegal for people under the age of sixteen to have sex. This is because you can't truly consent to having sex until you are mature enough to understand what it involves. The law is also there to protect you so that people can't make you do something you don't want to or aren't ready for.

No one should ever ask you to do anything sexual if you don't want to. If somebody is trying to persuade you against your will, make sure you speak to an adult straight away. If you don't feel like you can speak to anyone you know, a helpline such as Childline will help you (see page 154) or you can call the police.

When you're ready

Sex can be wonderful between consenting adults – it's a special way to show love when you are old enough and feel ready to. But I always think it's better to be aware and prepared for when it does happen. You'll learn more as you continue to grow up, but if you have any questions about it, speak to your parents or a teacher. Then, when you are finally ready, you'll know how to do it safely and responsibly!

BEAUTIFUL PEOPLE?

5

Yes! I've managed to get an Ed Sheeran song in too! Let me explain why ...

Like I've said before, human beings have an in-built need to connect with others. It's like a survival mechanism that's been hard-wired into us as we've evolved over thousands and thousands of years. When we were cavemen (and cavewomen), we would huddle in groups to interact and socialise. Now, we have the Internet!

The power of the web really came into its own when the
CORONAVIRUS CRISIS hit. All of a sudden we couldn't have as
much face-to-face contact, so the online world became hugely
important. I'll bet it's a big part of your life — it's definitely a
massive part of mine. In the time it's taken me to write the
opening of this chapter, I've sent an email, replied to some
tweets, checked my Instagram and ordered some food!

The Internet still blows my mind, because I can remember a
time before we had it (yes, I'm that old!). Now I can't imagine
life without it. I'm also guilty of spending a bit too much time
online to be honest, because it can be a big distraction (I've
just moved my phone away from me so I can get this chapter
done without looking at any more YouTube videos of dogs
on skateboards).

As much as I love the Internet, it can also be a place where we
need to look after ourselves. So, I'm always reminding people
to be careful when they're online, because it carries risks —
especially for young people. And let's not forget: that picture
on Instagram with one million likes? It might not even be real!
You might have noticed yourself that on social media people
sometimes look much better than they do in real life. What
we see online is often just a perfected version of what is
actually happening in reality. Most people aren't that beautiful
all the time!

That's why I've named this chapter after an **ED SHEERAN**
song. Did you know that Ed first became famous because of

the Internet? He started off performing on SBTV, a music channel on YouTube. His song 'Beautiful People' is about people who are out there showing off, looking glamorous, sporting their cars and designer clothes and going to glitzy parties. But everyday people don't live that way, and those social media celebs probably aren't always living the high life either. Social media and the Internet are not normal life. They're just people's edited best bits.

So in this chapter we're going to explore what the Internet is and the things that you need to be careful of. I'm not trying to be a party pooper! I just want you to get the most out of being online, but be safe doing it.

WHAT IS THE INTERNET?

You've grown up with it your whole life, but have you ever thought about what the Internet actually is?

The Internet lives on a network of machines that span across the globe called the 'World Wide Web'. These machines, or servers, hold all the information that you see online. Anyone with a computer or device connected to the Internet can access this network and see that information. You can also send (upload) information to the servers, as well as download it to store on your own device.

This has created an enormous online world where we can do everything from researching for homework, messaging friends and shopping, to watching our favourite films and shows, listening to music and posting a video of your **BUDGIE DOING SOMERSAULTS!** I must admit, I've got a bit obsessed with TikTok.

It also allows us to find out about what's going on in the world around us. To explore our dreams and interests. To learn more about who we are and who we'd like to be. For some, it's a place where they find help and support when they might be feeling sad or lonely. When you think about it, its capacity to improve our lives is truly awesome.

However, the Internet is a free-for-all. It can be used by anyone and anything can be put on it. Some apps and sites have people called moderators who check on things to make sure people don't post things that are false, offensive or unkind. However, not every website or app has that. And that means that, just like any superpower, the Internet can be used for good – or for evil.

And the riskiest part of it? You've guessed it. **SOCIAL MEDIA.**

SOCIAL MEDIA

Social media means any website or app which lets us connect, talk and share things, whether that's following your favourite celebrities, uploading your own pictures and videos, or keeping in touch with friends and family.

SOCIAL MEDIA IS HUGE! Did you know that Instagram has over a billion users? Reality TV star Kim Kardashian West has almost 200 million followers alone! That's more than twice the population of the whole United Kingdom! It can seem like social media is where everything is happening right now, which can be frustrating if you're not allowed on it yet. A lot of sites don't let you sign up unless you're over the age of thirteen. But try to be patient; these rules are designed to keep you safe online. Once you're ready to log on, always ask a parent or a carer before you sign up to a new account. When you do, it's probably a good idea to keep your settings as private as possible. And be extra careful if you're ever asked to enter payment information.

Filters

Filters might seem harmless on the surface,

but they can play havoc with our brains and self-esteem. That postcard-perfect holiday shot someone posted online? Probably not that idyllic in real life. Your favourite celebrity's latest glamorous selfie? THEY MAY HAVE CHANGED THE PHOTO so they look skinnier, more muscley or have perfect skin.

Even though you might think you're just having fun looking at all these pictures, subconsciously, your brain is comparing you and your life to the ones you're seeing online – and when you're up against a professionally filtered world, you're not going to come out on top. You wouldn't compare yourself to a Ken doll, because that's obviously fake. So why do it with pictures online?

Just bear this in mind the next time you see a post. Social media is not real life – it's a filtered version. Reminding yourself of this often and limiting the amount of time you spend looking at filtered pics are good ways to protect your self-confidence and body image (we talked about this in Chapter 1). So just remember: if you ever think: WOW! THAT LOOKS TOO GOOD TO BE TRUE … IT PROBABLY IS!

Fake news

Fake news is any type of news that's being reported as true but is actually made up, and it's rife on Twitter, Facebook and other social media sites. It's usually something shocking or a bit of gossip. Because the Internet is a place where you can pretty much write or say anything, fake news has been able to spread far and fast. There's an old saying, 'A lie can be halfway around the world while the truth is putting its boots on' – and that was way before the Internet was around! It's even quicker today. It can be pretty difficult to spot what's real and what's fake, especially because

we tend to trust stuff that seems to line up with what we already believe. And when we then share it with other people, we become part of the fake news problem ourselves.

If you want to avoid getting fooled, try to get your news from trustworthy websites. And before you share something, try searching for other online sources that back up its claims or that point out where it might be wrong.

Stay in control

DID YOU KNOW THAT ITS POSSIBLE TO BECOME ADDICTED TO SOCIAL MEDIA?

Research has shown that it stimulates the reward centres of our brains. This means that it feels good to use it, especially when you get 'likes' on one of your posts. For a small number of people, this can become addictive and they find it hard to log off because they constantly crave that buzz.

If you're worried about this, try the following:

1) Set yourself a time limit every day for how long you can be on social media. Apps such as Offtime can manage this for you.

2) When you're not using your device, make sure you're doing something to keep your brain occupied, such as a hobby or physical activity that you like. The more physical the better – you're less likely to pick up your device if your hands are busy!

3) Talk to an adult, and let them know what's happening.

MESSAGING

Messaging is a great way to stay in touch with others. You can send your mates a picture of what you're up to, or tell your parents where you are so they know you're safe. I prefer messaging because it means I don't have to spend ages talking on the phone to lots of different people.

However, there are some things that you need to be aware of when it comes to any kind of online messaging. The most important is that, whenever you send something in a message, you have no control over what happens to it next. People could forward it on or post it online. So be careful what you put out there.

If someone asks you to send them something – or are sending you sexual images – you should report it to an adult. Sending messages showing nudity or something sexual (known as sexting) is illegal for anyone under the age of 18 in the UK.

However, this isn't just about something sexual. If someone is messaging you and it's making you unhappy or uncomfortable in any way, or if you've sent something you're worried about, speak to someone you trust straight away. If you don't want to receive messages from a certain person, your messaging app probably has a way of blocking them. Have a look through the settings.

ONLINE PORN

Porn, or pornography, is material that contains explicit sexual content and aims to get people sexually excited. This is usually in the form of pictures or videos. You may have seen something on your friend's phone or computer. Since the dawn of the Internet, people have been able to access porn much more easily, and there's a lot more of it around.

Most people who look at porn are adults. However, over half of 11–13-year-olds have seen porn at some point, and the majority of them stumble across it by accident. Most young people who have seen it say that they don't like it – it can be upsetting or even frightening to see stuff you're not ready for.

To help ensure that you're only looking at stuff that's meant for your age, be extra-cautious around the choice of words you use when accessing a search engine to avoid seeing something unexpected. But if you do come across something by accident, don't panic. You haven't done anything wrong and the Internet police aren't about to appear, I promise. Either close your browser and start again, or just click 'back'.

Porn vs reality

One of the reasons why porn can be upsetting to look at is that sex between adults is rarely like what porn shows it to be. If you're curious about sex, porn isn't a good way of finding out more about what adults do in real life. Porn is made up and is often deliberately exaggerated – the noises are louder, the moves are more acrobatic and the language is more harsh. The actors are also chosen for their body types, and their body parts are often bigger than usual. Porn can also show relationships that aren't respectful or consenting, which is harmful, so it's probably not a good idea to copy or act out what you see in porn.

If you see something sexual online that worries or frightens you, it might be worthwhile speaking to an adult such as a teacher or family member about it.

CYBERBULLYING AND CYBER-SAFETY

It's just as important to stay safe online as it is in the real world. That means remembering a couple of pieces of advice.

BULLIES HANG OUT ONLINE TOO.

Bullying is unacceptable anywhere and that includes the web. Cyberbullying is the specific name given to bullying that takes place online. When it's on social media it's called trolling.

Nope, I'm not talking fairy-tale creatures who lurk under bridges. In this chapter, a troll is someone who posts offensive things about people on social media. Sadly, being behind a computer screen or smartphone rather than face-to-face means that people say more hurtful or outrageous things than they

ever would in real life. That goes for you too. Trolling can now also land you in big trouble with the law – so don't do it!

So before you comment on somebody else's post online, ask yourself these five things:
1) Is it relevant?
2) Is it necessary?
3) Is it helpful?
4) Is it fun?
5) Is it kind?
If it's not, then think twice about commenting!

>> HOW TO BEAT THE CYBERBULLIES

- Step away from your device or put it down. The online world is not your whole world – you have so much more!
- Change your privacy settings. You may be able to make your online profile more private so only your friends and family can see it and message you.
- If someone is attacking you online, try muting or blocking them. If what they are saying is serious, then make sure to also report them using the app's reporting function.
  - If all else fails, delete your online profile or account. You can always come back and start a new one.
  - If you are worried or upset at any time, make sure you speak to an adult about it. Never just keep it to yourself.

Protect yourself online

It's not just the trolls that you have to look out for. Remember that anyone you speak to online may not be who they seem, and may have different intentions to what you think. For example, catfishing is when someone tricks another person into becoming their friend or boyfriend/girlfriend by creating a fake online profile and pretending to be someone they're not. You may also have heard of grooming, where an adult deliberately manipulates a young person online with the aim of doing something sexual with them. This is illegal and should be reported as soon as possible.

That's why it's important to be cyber-savvy. Always be careful about who you are speaking to, and never give any personal information away unless you know it's someone you can trust. Likewise, never put your personal details on any websites, including your address or telephone number. I accidentally posted my email address on YouTube once … never again!

6

Want to feel good in three minutes flat? Then check out my favourite song by the gloriously fabulous Lizzo, 'Good as Hell'. Occasionally I'll be walking down the street with my headphones in and this song in my ears. I can't help but strut like I am the king (or queen) of the world! So like me, let's get you feeling good as hell too!

This chapter is all about how you can live your best life from the inside out. Right from the moment you open your sleep-heavy eyes in the morning, to when your head gladly hits the pillow at night, there are things you can do to make each day the best it can be.

Of course, not every day is going to be amazing. Some days you might feel like everything is pants. That's just how life is sometimes. But even on the tougher days, there is usually something you can do to make it a little bit easier.

We're going to start with how most of us begin our day: food!

EAT WELL

I am a massive foodie, and my ˙SWEET SPOT (ha!) is dessert.
I love it. However, as a doctor I know I should try to keep my
diet as balanced as possible.

Keeping things balanced means giving your body what it
needs, not just what you want. A balanced diet contains all
the right ingredients that our bodies require to perform their
necessary functions and to be as healthy as we can be. Just
like cars need fuel to run, our bodies need food to give them
energy and nutrients to do everything – including grow!

THE EATWELL GUIDE is a good example of what a balanced diet
looks like and was developed by experts in nutrition for the
UK after they looked at all the scientific evidence. It's a handy
visual guide to the sort of food we should be eating and how
much. There's loads of delicious stuff in there – take a look:

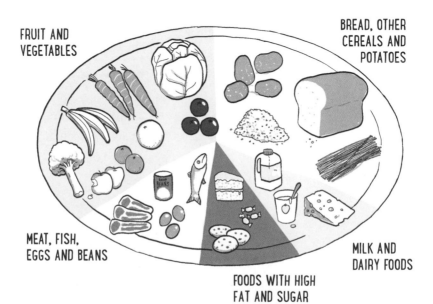

FRUIT AND
VEGETABLES

BREAD, OTHER
CEREALS AND
POTATOES

MEAT, FISH,
EGGS AND BEANS

FOODS WITH HIGH
FAT AND SUGAR

MILK AND
DAIRY FOODS

All food contains nutrients which our bodies need to do specific jobs. For example:

PROTEIN – This is the basic building block of all the cells in our bodies. It's especially important during growth when we are creating new cells. We can get protein from things such as meat, fish and eggs, or, if you are vegetarian or vegan, you can also get plenty from nuts, bread, tofu and lentils.

CARBOHYDRATE – This is the main source of our energy. Carbohydrates can be divided into two main types: simple (e.g. sugary and sweet stuff such as cakes, biscuits and chocolate) and complex (e.g. porridge, brown rice, peas and potatoes). Try to eat less of the simple carbs and more of the complex ones, as they give you energy for longer.

FAT – This has a really important role in the body because it forms part of our cells as well as being the way we store energy. Some food fats are good because they help keep us healthy (e.g. olive oil, avocado, nuts and oily fish), whereas others are not as helpful (e.g. pastries, fried food). Too much unhealthy fat can be bad in the long run.

VITAMINS AND MINERALS – These help our bodies work better in lots of different ways. For example, iron is important for our blood, we need calcium for our bones, vitamin C is good for healthy skin and a strong immune system, and vitamin D helps keep our bones strong. Fruit and vegetables are great sources of vitamins and minerals, as are cereals and milk.

WATER – Up to three-quarters of the human body is made up of water, so it's really important that we get enough of it. Staying hydrated keeps all the processes in our bodies working smoothly and helps our brains work better too.

Why is what we eat important?

That makes it sound like we only eat food to tick off a list of nutrients. Obviously that's not true – sitting down to eat some of your favourite foods, especially with people you love, is one of the best ways to relax and enjoy yourself. But there's no denying that what we eat can affect our health too.

Over one-third of young people aged ten or eleven are either overweight or obese. That means they are heavier than they ideally should be. It could make them more likely to develop health conditions in the long term, such as heart disease and type 2 diabetes. It can also affect the way they feel about themselves.

What we eat, how we feel and our body image (remember we talked about that in that in chapter one) are all linked to each other. Rather than focusing just on our weight or our size, we should be focusing on being healthy most of all, regardless of what we look like. Just as being very overweight may cause problems, so can being really underweight.

That's why I don't follow any fitness influencers on social

media. I don't have the time to spend my whole life exercising to look like they do – and besides, **THERE'S NO WAY I'M GOING TO SURVIVE ON EATING JUST BROCCOLI AND CHICKEN!** I like my cake too. So seeing their ripped abs and perfectly honed thighs isn't helpful for my body image – it just makes me feel like I'm not good enough.

I guess it's also because I've had a bit of a rocky relationship with food and weight. When I was a kid, I ate a lot of stuff that wasn't ideal, like crisps and chocolate etc. As a result, I was on the heavier side and that affected my confidence. I hated wearing shorts because I didn't like the way my legs looked. As a grown-up, I've been conscious of what I eat because of the same body-confidence issue, plus I know what it means for my health. So it can feel like a battle sometimes.

However, I make sure I remember that eating is absolutely necessary for life and shouldn't be seen as a bad thing.

If you are overweight and have been advised to try to get to a healthier weight, have a think about how you could make helpful changes to what you eat and do. However, don't stress over it and don't let anyone make you feel bad. Your happiness is not determined by how heavy you are. You will find what works for you in your own time.

There are some people who think a lot about what they are eating. This can go a bit too far. They become obsessed with it, particularly with controlling what they eat, or may be exercising a lot because they feel guilty about it. This might be the sign of something called an **EATING DISORDER**. If you find yourself being worried all the time about what you are eating, or cutting out a lot of food, or thinking about getting rid of the food you are given to eat, make sure you speak to an adult. You might need to see someone and get help.

Likewise, if you are thinking about losing weight, always speak to an adult about it first, such as a family member, someone at school or a health professional.

MOVE MORE

Everyone is always going on about how important **EXERCISE** is. You're probably sick of being told about it, to be honest. But do you know why it's so good for us?

It is great because it will:
1) Keep our bodies and hearts fit and healthy.
2) Keep our joints mobile.

3) Lower our risk of long-term health problems such as cancer, heart disease and type 2 diabetes.
4) Improve our mental health and help us feel good.
5) Improve how well we sleep.

Honestly, getting a bit of exercise in is the quickest mood-booster there is and will help you fall sound asleep at the end of the day rather than tossing and turning.

In the UK, the NHS advises that young people between the ages of five and eighteen do a mix of activities that get the heart pumping faster and ones that help make their muscles and bones stronger.

The current advice is to aim for at least sixty minutes of aerobic exercise a day. An hour every single day?! That might sound like a lot to you, but all of these things count, and I bet you're probably doing a few of them already:

- Walking to school or walking the dog
- Playing physical games at breaktime
- Cycling
- Skateboarding
- Riding a scooter.

Meanwhile, things that help strengthen your muscles and bones include:
- Playing a sport
- Running
- Dancing

- Gymnastics
- Swimming
- Martial arts.

At my school, we were made to do rugby, and I've got to admit, it wasn't really my thing. It didn't help that there was another boy in my year who was built like a **GIANT** and who had the same surname as me. Meanwhile, I was the shortest person in my class. You can probably guess what happened. Yep, the teachers kept getting us confused, and I would end up being made to play in the B-team, rather than the D-team. Let's just say I didn't enjoy being used as a rugby ball! I loved badminton though. So don't give up on sports too quickly – you probably just haven't found the right one for you yet.

There is nothing wrong with going to the gym if that's what you prefer. However, some gyms have rules about how old you have to be to go there. It's a good idea to be supervised by an adult so they can keep an eye on what you're doing and make sure you don't push yourself too hard and get injured. Plus it can take a while to learn how to use the equipment properly and safely.

Young people always want to use weights to help build their muscles. But weight-training when your

body is still growing may not be a good idea, because your muscles are a work-in-progress, and you're more likely to get injured. Until you're older – about sixteen – you're probably better off doing a variety of other things that you enjoy. Try the treadmill, cross trainer, rowing machine or the exercise bike.

You don't have to spend money or go to a gym to get healthy or fit though. There are groups and activities that you could explore at school or in your local community for free or very little.

I have to confess, I don't particularly like going to the gym. I find it really **BORING!** So between that and my experience of rugby at school, it's not a surprise to hear that for ages I thought of exercise as a chore – something I knew I had to do, but didn't enjoy. Then I discovered that I love dancing. I go to Zumba sessions and have even taken up bhangra classes. I've got so much fitter, and because I love doing it, it doesn't feel like exercise. Some people love football, or basketball, or swimming, and the fact that it keeps them fit is like a bonus on top.

The key is to find an activity or exercise that you enjoy doing, because you are so much more likely to keep it up.

THINK CLEARLY

The Brain

When you're going to school, cramming new information into your head every day, then looking after your brain is one of the best ways you can help yourself feel better. After all, school can be really tough, particularly if you have tests or exams. That's when you need to make sure you can learn and perform at your best.

It feels like I've done hundreds of exams: at school, at university and even since becoming a doctor. Along the way, I've discovered some handy tricks that can help keep your brain in **TIP-TOP** shape:

1) Get plenty of sleep: when you sleep, your brain sorts information out and stores what you need to remember. Making sure you get enough sleep is vital for learning – in fact, it's my No. 1 piece of advice.

2) Feed your brain: ensure that your brain has plenty of fuel to do all the things it needs to. Try to eat more healthily – aim for plenty of fruit and vegetables of different colours (that usually means they'll give you a mix of different nutrients), and drink enough water too.

3) Make a plan: if it's revision time, create a timetable to help you plan exactly what you're going to do and when. Some people prefer to study in the mornings, or if you're like me, you might be a night owl.

4) Give yourself a break: allow yourself short breaks during revision (e.g. around 15 minutes every hour or whatever works best for you). Some people revise in short bursts with lots of breaks, whilst others like to do mini marathons! Breaks are useful because it gives your brain a bit of a rest – in the long run, you'll take more in and it will stop you losing concentration entirely.

5) Stay away from stimulants: some people are tempted to drink caffeine-heavy things such as tea or coffee, or even take certain medicines, to keep them awake or help them to learn. These are a bad idea – don't forget, breaks and sleep

actually help your brain to work better – and can actually make things worse if you use them in the wrong way. Best to stay away from them unless you've been told to take them by a doctor.

If you're finding revision really tough, why not chat to one of your teachers to see if they can help you out? Or perhaps organise a homework or study club with your friends. There is nothing wrong with asking for advice or extra help – and not only could it make a real difference to your grades, it could also take the pressure off yourself.

What's the big deal about mental health?

In chapter two, we talked about **MENTAL HEALTH**. Having a healthy mind means we can do our day-to-day tasks and cope with any stresses in life. Good mental health also helps us have good relationships with friends and family, and perform well at school.

If you're feeling like you don't enjoy life, then it's vital that you get the help you need. There are loads of reasons why someone might struggle with their mental health.

Some people are just born with a higher chance of experiencing difficulty. There's not much you can do about that, but being aware of it means you can adopt good habits to help yourself. It can also be a response to something that's going on in your life, such as problems at home, school, bullying, stress, or the loss of a loved one. People who have long-term physical problems may experience mental-health issues as well.

EVERYONE EXPERIENCES MENTAL HEALTH DIFFERENTLY AND THEIR ABILITY TO COPE IS DIFFERENT TOO.

Here are some really simple things that you can do to boost your mental wellbeing:
- Try to eat as healthily as you can – a balanced diet will also make you feel good.
- Do some physical activity – whatever you can manage

is great. Exercise releases hormones called endorphins that make us feel good.

- Pay attention to sleep – better sleep means we cope with stress better too.
- Get outside – getting out and moving about is not only good for you physically, but also helps your mind! Try to get out in the fresh air as much as you can – go for a walk, run or play a sport.
- Be friendly – staying social changes our mood for the better. Check in with a mate to see how they are. What film did they watch last night? What music are they listening to? Even easy chat like this helps out our brains.
- Do things that make you feel good – such as watching a movie, or hanging out with friends or visiting your grandparents. Life shouldn't all be study, study, study! What do you enjoy doing?
- Speak to someone – if you're struggling, talking to someone about how you're feeling can really help. Chat with an adult you can trust.
- Keep a diary – if you find it hard to talk, writing your thoughts down gives you another outlet until you pluck up the courage for a conversation.
- Try some mindfulness.

What is mindfulness?

Mindfulness is a type of meditation. Basically, it involves concentrating on what you are feeling and experiencing right now. I find it helps me calm down if I'm feeling stressed and it stops me thinking and worrying about things that happened earlier in the day or what might happen tomorrow.

TRY OUT MY SIMPLE MINDFULNESS EXERCISE:

1) Sit somewhere comfortable and close your eyes.
2) Try to empty your mind and just concentrate on your breathing. Some people imagine their thoughts are like passing clouds that they are watching from afar.
3) Now imagine the air coming in via your nose, filling up your lungs, and then going out through your mouth. You don't have to breathe at a certain speed – whatever is comfortable. Some people like to picture their breath as a different colour coming in and going out. Whatever your trick, just focus on your breathing.
4) Do this for a few minutes. If your mind wanders, just bring it back to thinking about your breathing again.

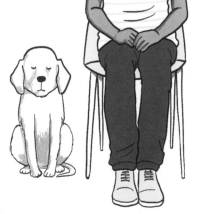

There are other mindfulness exercises you can try too. If you keep practising mindfulness, you should find that it gets easier. After a while you might notice that you can concentrate on things better and that you listen better too. Your mind slows down and you won't have so many thoughts racing around. It doesn't work for or help everyone though, so always ask for help if things are still difficult for you.

I sometimes feel really anxious, what can I do?

Anxiety is a big deal for many young people – and older ones. When coronavirus started to spread around the world, most of us had to stay at home. During this time many people started to experience anxiety for the first time, or it got worse. I think that's when people really started to take more notice of it.

I get anxiety sometimes too and have had to learn how to keep it under control. If you're getting anxious, mindfulness could help. We also talked about dealing with worry in Chapter 2.

However, sometimes anxiety can get so bad that you have a PANIC ATTACK. Panic attacks are a bit like your mind and body freaking out. You might feel really worried or sick. Your breathing might become fast and your heart beats faster and harder. You might also get headaches or stomach ache. They can make you feel quite unwell, but they will settle down and pass – they don't go on for ever.

Usually, a doctor or nurse will tell you if what you're having is a panic attack, so don't just assume. If it happens for the first time – get it checked!

If you are having panic attacks, or are getting really bad anxiety, why not try something called 'grounding'.

1) Take yourself somewhere quiet and sit on the ground.
2) Remind yourself that how you're feeling will pass and you will feel better again soon.
3) Look around you and name five things you can see.
4) Then name four things you can hear around you.
5) Then think of three things you can touch right now.
6) Then identify two things you can smell.
7) Finally, name one thing you can taste.

Hopefully, by the end of this you should be feeling much calmer.

Looking out for others

Just as we should all look out for ourselves and our own mental health, it's good to look out for others too.

If you're worried about a friend or family member and you think they might be going through a tough time, try to help if you can. Many people worry about how to do this, but my advice is:

1) Ask if they're OK.
2) Let them speak and listen to what they're saying. They may not want to tell you anything serious straight away, but let them know you're there if they want to talk, or that you can get someone else for them if they prefer.
3) Be kind and give them a helping hand. This could be something simple such as involving them in activities so they feel more included, or offering to help them revise for an upcoming test.
4) Speak to an adult if you're really worried about someone. It's always best to do this with the person's agreement if you can.

Anyone could end up in a situation where they need a listening ear and a helping hand, so try to look out for others just like you'd want them to look out for you.

DON'T FORGET THE LITTLE GUYS

Dot the 'I's ...

Your eyes are an incredible bit of body equipment. Did you know that they don't actually grow in size as you grow? They pretty much stay the same size from when you are a baby to when you're fully mature. Plus, the muscles that move them are some of the fastest in the human body. And they're able to see about one million different colours. I think they deserve looking after! Looking after your eyes also means that you can do better at school, because **VISION IS HELPFUL FOR LEARNING**.

Some tips on keeping them working at their best include:
1) If you're doing any reading, make sure the room is well lit so you don't strain too much to see.
2) Try not to stare at the same thing for long periods of time (such as screens). Give your eyes regular breaks.
3) If you're out in bright, sunny weather, wear sunglasses to protect your eyes.
4) Have regular eye checks by an optician. If you've been given glasses, make sure you wear them!

Cross the 'Ts ...

Smiles are super important so don't forget to brush your teeth! I know this sounds obvious, but trust me: you'd be amazed how many people don't look after them and end up having them removed in my hospital.

- Brush them every night before you go to sleep and at least once more at another time of day – most kids do this in the morning before going to school.
- Every time you brush, make sure you get to each and every tooth and all surfaces.
- Brush for at least two minutes.
- Use a brush that's the right size for your mouth. If it's too big, you might struggle to get it around all the nooks and crannies.
- Use a toothpaste that contains fluoride. This helps to keep your teeth strong. But only use the recommended amount.
- After brushing, don't rinse your mouth out with water – just spit out the toothpaste. Whatever's left in your mouth helps to protect your teeth while you sleep.

Remember to see a dentist regularly. They can check your teeth and give you more advice on looking after them. (Super-obvious tip: avoiding too many sweet things and sugary drinks will keep your teeth nice and healthy.)

If you wear braces, it's particularly important to listen to what your dentist says because they need special attention. Fortunately, even if you hate having them, they won't be on forever, and just think of how awesome your teeth will be once they're off.

SLEEP SOUNDLY

Sleep is possibly one of the most vital things our bodies and brains do, but we always forget how important it is. In fact, it's often the first thing that we scrimp on. How many times have you stayed up late and then regretted it in the morning?

Think of sleep as food for the brain. Getting enough sleep is important because:

- It helps your brain sort out information it's taken in during the day and decide what to store as memories.
- It's the time when your body repairs itself and grows.
- It improves your concentration during the day so you can learn more.
- It improves your ability to deal with stress.

- It boosts your mood and mental health.
- It improves your physical performance so you have more energy and can do more.
- It helps your immune system so you are better at fighting off illnesses.
- It reduces your chances of developing conditions such as obesity, heart disease and cancer.

SEE? SLEEP IS PHENOMENAL.

How much sleep you need depends on how old you are. For example, babies need a lot more sleep than adults because they do so much growing in a short space of time. A young person needs something in between. Everyone is different, but as a general rule, the average 8–12-year-old needs around ten hours every night, and teenagers need around nine hours.

How do you know if you're getting enough? Well, a simple way of telling is to see how you feel in the middle of the morning. If you're still feeling really tired, then you probably need a bit more sleep the next night!

As you enter your teenage years, your sleep patterns change. You'll go from wanting to go to bed and waking up early to finding it harder to go to sleep and then not wanting to leave your bed in the morning. This is a temporary phase, but it is a real thing that happens to your body – it's not just you being lazy, whatever your parents say! You can always reassure them by telling them your sleep patterns will change again as you get older so that you're able to go to bed and get up at a 'more reasonable' time!

How can I make my sleep better?

Sleep problems are actually quite common in young people. Usually the solution is quite simple and can be sorted out at home. Here are my tips if you're struggling to snooze:

1) Try to go to bed and wake up at a similar time every day. This gets your body into a pattern.

2) Have a wind-down routine every night before you go to sleep. For example, have a bath and read a book.

3) Have a power-down hour: try not to use any electronic devices in the hour before bed. These can interfere with the chemicals in our brains that help us sleep.

4) Make sure your bedroom is as sleep-friendly as possible: it should be warm, dry, dark, quiet and comfortable.

5) Try not to eat or drink too close to bedtime, especially anything that has caffeine in it (e.g. tea, coffee, cola) as this can keep you awake.

BUZZING

Choc

If you are still finding it really difficult then you might have to speak to a doctor about it, as you may need professional help (obviously speak to a parent or carer first).

OH MY GOD. I'VE WET THE BED!

You might think you're way too old for this, but I know from being a doctor that MANY YOUNG PEOPLE STILL WET THE BED NOW AND AGAIN. It can happen for lots of reasons – the most common being simply that you didn't go for a pee before getting into bed or you drank too much close to bedtime! However, it can also happen if you have an infection in your urine, if your bladder is playing up and not holding your urine properly, or if your body isn't sensing that you need to pee and waking you up in time.

If bedwetting is something new for you or it keeps happening, then you may need to see a doctor. Don't feel embarrassed: I promise it's much more common than you might think, and often there's a simple solution.

OUT IN THE REAL WORLD

One of the amazing things that happens as you grow up is you gradually get more independence. You're spending less time with your parents and more time on your own, or just with your mates. It feels brilliant – but it also means you've got to be more responsible.

If I'm honest, **I WAS A BIT OF A GOODY-GOODY** when I was your age. I definitely wasn't perfect, but I hardly did anything naughty. That wasn't the case for my brother, who was the complete opposite of me. He'd get in trouble all the time.

As we learned in chapter two, as we grow up we start to take more risks. This is perfectly normal stuff. The problem is that it happens at the same time as we begin to face new temptations and challenges in the real world. Sometimes the choices we make may not be great and could land us in trouble.

This is especially the case when it comes to things such as drugs, alcohol and smoking.

Drugs, legal highs and alcohol

It's not unusual for young people to experiment with alcohol, drugs or 'legal highs' as they're growing up. Often this is because their friends

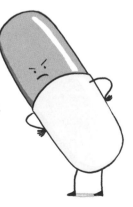

are doing the same and they feel like they have to – peer pressure in action (see page 80). However, these substances could do serious harm to you.

The laws around drugs and alcohol are confusing, so let's break it down so you have the facts. In the UK, you have to be over eighteen to buy alcohol, though you can drink it when you're younger as long as you're doing it with family.

DOING DRUGS IS ALWAYS ILLEGAL AT ANY AGE. Legal highs are chemicals that can affect how you feel, but aren't illegal because they're actually designed to be used for something else. That doesn't mean they're not dangerous. A classic example is 'laughing gas' or 'nitrous oxide'. We use this in hospitals to help people with pain, but it gets misused to get a 'high', especially at festivals, and can make people really unwell.

Alcohol reduces your inhibitions and you become more likely to make bad decisions or take serious risks, whether it's staying out too late and not having a way to get home or not being careful around busy roads. It can also make you really sick – if you drink too much, you can end up in hospital. Drugs and legal highs can be very bad for you too. My advice: drink responsibly (if you want to) when you are old enough to do it, and don't take any drugs!

Smoking and vaping

Smoking is, thankfully, becoming less and less common among young people. Smoking cigarettes causes serious health problems and has resulted in a huge number of premature deaths. It not only damages your lungs (and can cause things such cancer), but it can also give you problems with your heart. Plus it's really addictive and difficult to quit once you start, so best to avoid altogether.

VAPING, on the other hand, seems to be growing in popularity. Rather than using cigarettes, when you vape you inhale a vapour from a small electronic device. They can seem pretty tempting, because they come in all sorts of different flavours and all the adverts say it's better for you than smoking.

WHILE VAPES MIGHT BE LESS HARMFUL THAN CIGARETTES THEYRE STILL NOT IDEAL.

These devices are so new that we don't know what long-term effects they might have. Vaping can be a good way for addicted people to come off cigarettes, but shouldn't be taken up for any other reason.

My advice: you're better off without smoking and vaping – plus they cost you a lot of money. Save your cash for something better!

HOW TO GROW UP AND FEEL AMAZING!

This is it, the end of the book. But this is really just the start of your amazing journey of growing up and figuring out who you are. You have so much more to learn and do. However, I'm hoping that these chapters have given you some decent information and advice to use along the way.

We've talked about the changes your body and mind are going through, and how to look after them. We've explored the relationships you are already in and will be having with other people, and how to make the most of them. We've covered sex and more grown-up stuff. We've looked at the awesome online world and how you can be a safe part of it. And finally, we've learned about how you really can live your best life every day. **PHEW!**

When I started thinking about what I wanted to put in this book, I wanted it to be the book that I needed when I was growing up. A one-stop-shop to help me understand what was going on with me, and that made me more prepared to face the world around me.

Let's be honest, though. There's no way we could have covered absolutely everything, As I said, this is just a starting point. Now it's over to you.

It's quite likely that there are issues that are still confusing you. Or you may have more questions. That's why I've continually said – until you're sick of reading it – to ask an adult if you're worried about anything, or to check out some of the many sources of information I've listed in the Resources section which comes straight after this chapter.

If you still feel like you need a road map to get a handle on growing up, **YOU'RE NOT ALONE**. This is a pretty overwhelming time. So my final piece of advice is try and learn from other people. This is why we have role models – people you look up to that inspire you. They could be someone on TV, online, or a person you know in real life. Role models are people that make you think: one day, I want to be like you.

One of my role models was the character Dr Doug Ross in the American TV show ER (played by actor George Clooney). He was smart and funny – and also really good at his job, especially in an emergency. Because guess what? He was an emergency paediatrician, like I am today. Sadly, I'm not as funny as he was, but hey, you can't have everything! Your role model doesn't have to be someone who has the job of your dreams, but if you like their attitude to life, their values or their mad dance skills, then emulating them can help you figure out how to be your best self.

Your role model might shift over time too, because our hopes, dreams and goals will change as we grow up. How you feel now will be different to how you'll feel in a few years' time. Go with the flow, use the advice you have found in this book and from others, and see how things unfold – that's the exciting part!

After all, while it's always important to take guidance from those around you and benefit from their experience and advice, at the end of the day, you determine who you are, how you'll live your life as an adult, and what your mantra will be.

'ERM, YOUR WHAT, RANJ?'

A mantra is a motto that you live your life by. Why not have one too? Mine is:

DREAM BIG.
WORK HARD.
BE KIND.

They're basically the rules I try to follow every day.

I grew up with very little, and dreaming big helped to remind me that things could be amazing later on. However, that wasn't going to happen if I didn't put the work in. I had to knuckle down and work hard to get through school and university, to become a doctor and work in TV, and then to achieve some dreams I never thought would come true! Honestly, all that hard work was worth it.

Along the way, I have always tried to be kind. First, being nice is always easier and more helpful than being mean. If you're kind to others, hopefully they'll help you out when you need it – and I haven't got to where I am today all by myself. Secondly, I realised that it's vital to be kind to yourself. **WERE ONLY HUMAN, AND WE CAN ONLY DO SO MUCH AT ONE TIME**. When you recognise that you can't do everything all at once and that you won't always get it right, you give yourself a break and take some of the pressure off.

Using my mantra to guide how I live has got me to where I am now. It's helped me to realise who I am and what matters to me. It's allowed me to be confident in myself and to have wonderful relationships with others. It's given me a life that I love. And most of all, it's enabled me to feel proud of who I am.

So here's where I let you go off and become your amazing self too. Don't worry, you've got this! I've got every faith in you and I know you'll be fine. Think of all the things you've learned in this book. Take a deep breath, remember the stuff I've told you and take your first step on the journey to growing up. And if you ever find yourself having a bit of a wobble, don't forget to look out of the window before you go to sleep at night. How ridiculously incredible is it that you are made of star stuff? Proof, if you needed any, that you are already amazing.

Ranj's Ultimate Growing-Up Playlist

'WHO YOU ARE' – JESSIE J

'THIS IS ME' – KEALA SETTLE AND THE GREATEST SHOWMAN ENSEMBLE

'HAKUNA MATATA' – THE LION KING

'I'LL BE THERE FOR YOU' – THE REMBRANDTS

'LET'S TALK ABOUT SEX' – SALT-N-PEPA

'BEAUTIFUL PEOPLE' – ED SHEERAN

'GOOD AS HELL' – LIZZO

Resources

NHS https://www.nhs.uk
The NHS website has a complete A to Z on health conditions, including mental health. It also has links to further help in case you need more. It's mainly aimed at adults, but the stuff on there is useful for younger people too.

Eatwell Guide https://www.nhs.uk/live-well/eat-well/the-eatwell-guide
Info on the NHS Eatwell Guide to healthy, balanced eating.

Kids Health https://kidshealth.org
An American website which aims to help kids, teens and their parents take charge of their health. There's lots of stuff on physical and mental health on there.

Childline https://www.childline.org.uk
0800 1111
Childline is run by the charity NSPCC and helps anyone under the age of nineteen. There's information and advice on everything from friends and relationships to home and school life. You can also get support with their 1-2-1 chat online or you can call the helpline.

Young Minds https://youngminds.org.uk
Young Minds is one of the main mental health charities for young people. You can find help on lots of mental wellbeing topics and there is also a dedicated helpline for parents and carers.

Anti-bullying alliance https://www.anti-bullyingalliance.org.uk
This site includes loads of information on bullying and how to deal with it, including info on your rights and the law.

Ditch the Label https://www.ditchthelabel.org
An international anti-bullying charity for anyone aged 12 to 25 who needs help with things such as bullying, confidence, self-esteem or coming out.

Just Like Us https://www.justlikeus.org
A charity for young people that aims to promote diversity in schools. Each year they run a school Diversity Week.

ERIC https://www.eric.org.uk
The leading bladder and bowel charity for children and young people. They have information for kids and teens who might have any toilet-related issues, including bedwetting.

FRANK https://www.talktofrank.com
Up-to-date and straightforward information on drugs and alcohol. It's mainly aimed at older kids and teens.

ROSPA https://www.rospa.com
The go-to charity for advice on accidents, injuries and staying safe for the whole family.

The following free apps are endorsed by the NHS and can be used by young people:

NHS Go
Confidential health advice for young people.

MeeTwo
A safe place for teens to discuss any issue affecting their lives.

Brush DJ
Helps young people to better care for their teeth in a fun way.

Chill Panda
Learn breathing techniques to help relax and deal with stress and worry.

Glossary

acne: Red, oily spots on the face or body that happen during puberty.

Adam's apple: Part of the voice box that sticks out in the neck and gets bigger during puberty.

aerobic exercise: Any exercise that involves moving around and making your heart beat faster.

amygdala: Part of the brain that is involved in experiencing emotions.

asexual: Someone who doesn't feel sexually attracted to anyone.

bisexual: Someone who feels sexually attracted to both the same sex and the opposite sex.

blended family: A family made up of two parents and their children from previous relationships.

body image: What you see when you look at yourself and how it makes you feel.

bystander: A person who is present during something but doesn't take part.

carbohydrate: A group of nutrients in food, including sugars, that the body uses for energy.

catfishing: Pretending to be someone you are not online to trick or fool someone else.

circumcision: Process of removing the foreskin in boys.

concussion: An injury to the brain when you bump your head.

consent: Permission to do something, e.g. before having sex with someone.

contraception: Something that prevents a woman getting pregnant from sex.

eating disorder: An abnormal way of eating, thinking about or behaving around food that causes you harm.

egg: Special cells released from women's ovaries every month that help to make a baby.

ejaculation: When sperm is released from a boy's body during sexual activity.

endorphins: Chemicals produced by the body that make you feel good.

erection: When a boy's penis becomes stiff, usually during sexual activity.

fake news: Online news that is not true, but is being reported as if it is.

fat: A type of nutrient in food that is also a way that the body stores energy.

fluoride: A mineral that makes teeth stronger. It's sometimes added to toothpaste.

forebrain: Part of the brain that deals with higher functions such as complex thoughts and personality.

foreplay: Any sexual activity between two people that gets them excited before sex.

gender: The sex that you identify with (e.g. male or female).

genitals: Sexual organs on the outside of the body of a boy or girl.

grooming: When an adult deliberately manipulates a young person with the aim of assaulting or abusing them.

growing pains: Unexplained aches and pains in the legs that children get when growing up.

heterosexual: Someone who is sexually attracted to someone of the opposite sex.

homosexual: Somebody who is sexually attracted to someone of the same sex.

hormones: Chemicals produced by the body that are important in things such as growth and puberty.

identity: Who you are or what you feel like (e.g. gender: male or female).

labia: The folds of skin on the body that cover the opening of a girl's vagina.

legal high: Substance that affects the way you think and mimics the effects of illegal drugs.

lesbian: A girl that is sexually attracted to another girl.

LGBT+: A collective term used to describe people who are not 'straight' or heterosexual (e.g. lesbian, gay, bisexual, transgender and others).

masturbation: Rubbing or touching sexual organs for pleasure.

menstrual cup: Small cup that is inserted into the vagina to collect a period and is then cleaned out and replaced.

menstrual cycle: Monthly cycle of a girl's uterus that makes pregnancy possible (or ends in a period).

mental health: A term used to describe the health or wellbeing of the mind.

nerve cell: Type of cell that carries electrical signals and forms part of the brain or nervous system.

orgasm: Intense feeling of pleasure that usually happens during ejaculation.

panic attack: Sudden episode of fear or anxiety that can also have physical symptoms.

peer pressure: Feeling of pressure to do something because of someone else.

penile papules: Small, harmless spots on the glans of the penis.

period: Release of blood from a girl's uterus out of her vagina when the lining is shed.

pores: Tiny openings in the skin that release oils and sweat.

pornography: Material showing sexual activity (in print, on-screen or online) that is used to get excited.

premenstrual syndrome (PMS): Unpleasant feelings or moods that girls get just before their periods.

puberty: Physical changes that happen when you are growing from a child into an adult.

pubic hair: Hair on the genitals that develops during puberty.

safe/safer sex: Using contraception during sexual intercourse to prevent unwanted pregnancy or STIs.

sanitary pad: A pad that girls put inside their underwear to collect any fluids such as discharge or periods.

sebum: Oily fluid released through the skin pores.

semen: Whitish-yellow fluid that contains sperm from the testicles.

sex: The gender you are born with (male or female), or a word to describe any sexual activity or sexual intercourse.

sexting: Sending a message that contains sexual language or pictures.

sexual intercourse: Sexual activity between two people, usually involving the genitals.

smegma: Whitish-yellowy stuff that collects under a boy's foreskin.

sperm: Special cells made by a boy's testicles that help to make babies.

STI: Sexually transmitted infection, or an infection that is spread through sexual activity.

tampon: A small plug that is placed inside a girl's vagina to soak up blood from a period.

transgender: Someone that identifies as a different gender to the one they were born.

trolling: Type of online bullying where someone posts mean comments or attacks someone else.

wet dream: A sexual dream where the person might orgasm (and ejaculate) during their sleep.

Index

Acknowledgements

Where do I start? There are so many amazing people who have helped this book become what it is, that I barely know where to begin! I want you all to know that I appreciate each and every one of you.

I have to say a huge thank you to the team at Hachette who took a chance on me and gave me this great opportunity – especially Liza Miller whom I could not have done this without! You helped me find a voice and for that I will always be grateful. Thanks also to the rest of the team: Sadie Smith, Laura Hambleton, Debbie Foy, Emma Blackburn, Nicola Goode, Dominic Kingston and James McParland, who have all been so wonderful to work with.

Massive thanks has to go out to the illustrator, David O'Connell, for bringing my ideas to life in such a beautiful way. You really hit the nail on the head!

Thank you to my management team: my friends, guides and rocks. To Craig Latto, who somehow always knows what I'm thinking and is quite possibly the best agent I could ever have. To Jamie Brenner, for whom no task is too big or too small, and I can always rely on. And to dear KT Forster, who never gave up on me and made sure that my writing demons didn't get the better of me. Our chats over countless cups of tea were the lifeblood of this book, and your precious advice gave me confidence when I really needed it. Also thank you to Maisy Tindle for checking over the chapter about the Internet. Your feedback was great!

I have to give a mention to all my incredible NHS colleagues here. Thank you for constantly reminding me of what matters and for keeping me grounded. Especially my wonder-women Tanya Gill and Miriam Fine-Goulden. Your friendship and support never go unnoticed, and you inspire me every day. You have been my champions, and I will forever be yours.

Last, but by no means least, I want to express my endless gratitude to my friends and family. I've told you countless times before, and I'll say it again: you are the reason I can do what I do. Your kindness means everything. Especially Emma Morris who has been my confidante, conscience and wing-woman throughout this. I am beyond lucky to have you as my friend. And my dance partner for life, Janette. So much of what you have taught me is in this book – love ya, honey!

Growing up, I didn't ever think I would one day be doing something like this. This is truly a dream-come-true for me, and I'm still pinching myself! That little boy who just wanted to be happy, but kept everything buried deep inside, has finally been given a chance to speak. I wrote this for you. I want you to know that you are awesome, no matter what.

And please, don't worry. It gets better.

R x

Acknowledgements

Where do I start? There are so many amazing people who have helped this book become what it is, that I barely know where to begin! I want you all to know that I appreciate each and every one of you.

I have to say a huge thank you to the team at Hachette who took a chance on me and gave me this great opportunity – especially Liza Miller whom I could not have done this without! You helped me find a voice and for that I will always be grateful. Thanks also to the rest of the team: Sadie Smith, Laura Hambleton, Debbie Foy, Emma Blackburn, Nicola Goode, Dominic Kingston and James McParland, who have all been so wonderful to work with.

Massive thanks has to go out to the illustrator, David O'Connell, for bringing my ideas to life in such a beautiful way. You really hit the nail on the head!

Thank you to my management team: my friends, guides and rocks. To Craig Latto, who somehow always knows what I'm thinking and is quite possibly the best agent I could ever have. To Jamie Brenner, for whom no task is too big or too small, and I can always rely on. And to dear KT Forster, who never gave up on me and made sure that my writing demons didn't get the better of me. Our chats over countless cups of tea were the lifeblood of this book, and your precious advice gave me confidence when I really needed it. Also thank you to Maisy Tindle for checking over the chapter about the Internet. Your feedback was great!

I have to give a mention to all my incredible NHS colleagues here. Thank you for constantly reminding me of what matters and for keeping me grounded. Especially my wonder-women Tanya Gill and Miriam Fine-Goulden. Your friendship and support never go unnoticed, and you inspire me every day. You have been my champions, and I will forever be yours.

Last, but by no means least, I want to express my endless gratitude to my friends and family. I've told you countless times before, and I'll say it again: you are the reason I can do what I do. Your kindness means everything. Especially Emma Morris who has been my confidante, conscience and wing-woman throughout this. I am beyond lucky to have you as my friend. And my dance partner for life, Janette. So much of what you have taught me is in this book – love ya, honey!

Growing up, I didn't ever think I would one day be doing something like this. This is truly a dream-come-true for me, and I'm still pinching myself! That little boy who just wanted to be happy, but kept everything buried deep inside, has finally been given a chance to speak. I wrote this for you. I want you to know that you are awesome, no matter what.

And please, don't worry. It gets better.

R x